What people are sa
and *Igni..* .., ...

"David Yanez is a man whom God has raised up to bring heaven's glory and miracle-working power on earth. He is on the cutting edge of ministry and hungry to see people changed by God's miracle working power. God has performed many outstanding miracles in his ministry. His book contains great revelation knowledge. As you read his book, you will find spiritual enrichment and a desire to join him in doing the works of Jesus."

—*Dr. Gary Wood*
Author, *A Place Called Heaven*

"David Yanez has been gifted by God to expand vision to those who call on the name of the Lord. In *Igniter of Faith*, he leads you, in laymen's terms with the revelation of the Holy Spirit, in how to move in the spiritual gift of miracles. This is a must read for beginning missionaries and anyone who desires to be used in the realm of the miraculous."

—*Bishop Mike Renteria*
Kingdom Faith Church, Elsa, Texas
Author, *Old Man Versus New Man* and *Understanding the Spiritual Realm*

"*Igniter of Faith* is, hands down, one of the best books ever written on the subject of faith. This powerful revelation enables people from any walk of life to build their faith to the point of experiencing their miracle. You must get your copy today!"

—*Darrell McManus*
Founder, Darrell McManus Ministries
Author, *12 Spirits Seducing the Church* and *What You Didn't Know about God's Throne*

"*Igniter of Faith* includes a lion's share of testimonies and biblical references, but what I find most convincing is that David is not just relaying information he may have discovered in his research; he is a crusade evangelist who turns the reader into a firsthand witness of the miracles and healings of God he has experienced in many of his miraculous church meetings and conferences, both in the US and overseas. I highly recommend this book for anyone who has been praying for the spiritual gifts of healing and miracles—ministry professionals and laity alike. I also recommend this book for believers who need a practical understanding of these spiritual gifts."

—*Frank Mazzapica*
Pastor, New Covenant Church, Humble, Texas
Author, *The Unsupervised Man, The Unsupervised Woman, The Touch-Me-Not Woman,* and *Putting Pants Back On the Church*

"*Igniter of Faith* is one of the most informative and faith-building books I have ever read. I would recommend this book to pastors, Christians, and even non-believers. It will inspire your faith and teach you how to receive miracles. David Yanez is a man of faith, greatly used of God in the healing and miracle ministry. His teachings and experiences will bring you to a different level of faith. He has a true ministry of reaching the unreachable for the kingdom of God."

—*Pastor Jack Wells*
Christian Fellowship Church, Denham Springs, Louisiana

"*Igniter of Faith* will help anyone seeking a miracle to receive what they need from God. It is both practical and insightful, expounding the Word of God with clarity and power. But this book will not only help those who need a touch from God for themselves, it will empower every preacher who wants to know how to bring the atmosphere of heaven to earth. It will give leaders the tools they need to operate effectively in the Spirit to release God's power in the lives of His people."

—*Jo Naughton*
Pastor, Harvest Church, London, England
Author, *30-Day Detox for Your Soul*

"David Yanez takes us on a journey over the past five years of his ministry experiences in Africa, India, and the US. Using anecdotes of his first-hand experiences, along with applicable Scripture, he explains how healing works. *Igniter of Faith* gives the reader an illuminating insight into practical ministry; how to stand in faith believing, often despite what we see. God is always faithful to answer our prayers of faith."

—*Peter Stanway*
The Way Christian Ministries, Mijas, Spain
Author, *Boys from Glasgow Don't Cry* and *Who Is McKenzie?*

"*Igniter of Faith* is filled with Scripture, wisdom, incredible stories of personal encounters with the Holy Spirit and the power of God, and amazing insight on how to keep the flames of faith burning. As I read it, I was challenged to pursue more of the Holy Spirit, to increase my expectations of God's power, and to stand more firmly on the written Word. If David can see the mighty miracles he writes about, you can see them, too! This is a great book to challenge any believer to greater heights and glories."

—*Dan Armstrong*
Pastor, Genesis Ministries, Canyon Lake, Texas
Author, *Following the Still Small Voice*

"It was so invigorating to my heart and to my faith to read *Igniter of Faith*. The illustrations of so many healings and miracles will stir faith in the heart of any reader. I received a phone call as I was nearing the end of the book. A dear friend since childhood was in need of healing from an unidentifiable infection. Full of faith from reading this book's reports of miracles, I offered a strong prayer with renewed confidence of God's healing power. David Yanez has inspired my faith anew. I love it!"

—*Gerald Davis*
Gerald Davis Ministries, Conroe, Texas
Author, *Crown of Thorns* and
How to Function in This Economy

"Operating in miracles is part of our inheritance as children of God. *Igniter of Faith* helps believers receive the full revelation that miracles are for all hurting people while we are on this earth. The message contained in this book will help you to ignite faith for your miracle, and for miracles in the lives of others."

—*David Hope*
Pastor, Words of Life Church, Humble, Texas
Author, *Inhabiting Eternity on Earth* and *Keep Knocking*

IGNITER *of* FAITH

DAVID YANEZ

WHITAKER
HOUSE

Igniter of Faith:
Release Your Miracle

David Yanez Ministries
PO Box 5172
Kingwood, TX 77325
www.davidyanezministries.com
david@davidyanezministries.com

ISBN: 978-1-62911-559-7
eBook ISBN: 978-1-62911-581-8
Printed in the United States of America
© 2015 by David Yanez

Whitaker House
1030 Hunt Valley Circle
New Kensington, PA 15068
www.whitakerhouse.com

Library of Congress Cataloging-in-Publication Data

Yanez, David, 1971–
  Igniter of faith : release your miracle / by David Yanez.
      pages cm
  ISBN 978-1-62911-559-7 (trade pbk. : alk. paper) — ISBN 978-1-62911-581-8 (ebook) 1. Miracles. 2. Spiritual healing. 3. Healing—Religious aspects—Christianity. 4. Yanez, David, 1971– I. Title.
  BT97.3.Y36 2015
  231.7'3—dc23
                                    2015029043

1 2 3 4 5 6 7 8 9 10 11 LJ 22 21 20 19 18 17 16 15

DEDICATION

I dedicate this to my father, Reverend Gabriel Yanez Jr., who passed away too early but built a home full of faith in God and gave his family a belief in miracles.

"Then shall thy light break forth as the morning, and thine health shall spring forth speedily: and thy righteousness shall go before thee; the glory of the Lord *shall be thy rearward."*
—Isaiah 58:8

CONTENTS

FOREWORD

We live in a time of great confusion, turmoil, and brokenness. Never before has the world seemed more troubled and in need of a demonstration of God's loving power through healing, signs, and wonders. The gospel of Jesus Christ is the power of God unto salvation, and when it is presented in faith, it has the power to heal any sickness, to deliver anyone from demons, and to save anyone, no matter how evil their past. The power of God Almighty is released through the preaching of the gospel by those who believe. Its strength is unstoppable, its passion is unrelenting, and its truth cannot be defeated by human reasoning. Our God is a God of love, but He is also a mighty God.

We will not apologize for the demands that the gospel places on people, nor will we ever be ashamed of its message. It is essential that all who call Jesus Christ their Lord stand fast on His Word and proclaim His truth with passion and faith, trusting Him to confirm His message with signs and wonders. As sons of God, we cannot compromise the gospel message to avoid offending those who hate the truth and love evil. Our Lord came into this world in the form of a servant to fulfill all righteousness and to destroy the works of the devil. One day, the Lion of the tribe of Judah will return to earth to rule with an iron rod as the King of Kings and Lord of Lords; and it is my hope that when He does, He will receive the full reward for His earthly sufferings: billions of souls who have been washed by His shed blood and healed by His broken body. Until He returns, you and I are His witnesses and the instruments through which He releases His power to save, heal, and deliver. We must be willing to speak on His behalf and to trust Him to act upon His message.

I want to challenge you to read *Igniter of Faith* and ask God to release in you the same passion for God and for the salvation of the lost that David Yanez possesses. Soak in this book and allow its atmosphere of faith to become your lifestyle, and his vision your joy.

—*Joan Hunter*
Author and healing evangelist
www.joanhunter.org

INTRODUCTION

I hope to create in my readers a higher expectation of healing and miracles in their lives by the end of reading this book. God wants all of us, young and old, to believe that He can perform what's written in His Word. Most importantly, He wants you to know that miracles and healings are available for such a time as today. Miracles are needed in the world today like never before. People often ask me why God does amazing miracles in my ministry in India. I tell them that, in a nation where the people serve over one million gods, the one true, living God likes to flex His muscles in healings and miracles.

Throughout this book, you will read amazing stories of my own firsthand experiences of miracles over many years. The most recent miracle stories are from my mission trips to India and Africa over the past five years. I will take you on a journey of faith through this book with Scriptures, true stories, and personal experiences that will ignite your faith. You will learn how to change the atmosphere around you into an atmosphere of faith. You will learn that there is a time and a place for creative miracles. You will learn about the power of compassion in releasing miracles. You will also learn how to release miracles for others as an igniter of faith. You will gain a deeper revelation of working in the healing ministry. You will also have the understanding of God's will for miracles and healings in your life. My prayer is that after reading this book, you, too, will be used by God in miracles and healing!

CHAPTER 1

JESUS, THE ORIGINAL HEALING EVANGELIST

Igniting the Atmosphere for Miracles to Happen

Over the years, I have studied great men of faith who held healing campaigns. In each of their services, there was an expectation in the atmosphere. People went to the services expecting a miracle. The videos of the great A. A. Allen, Oral Roberts, Jack Coe, and Morris Cerullo are truly inspiring. These men had such electricity in the way that they progressed a room in faith. To them, it was never about just preaching a sermon to the crowds. These men of God took people on a journey to another place in the Spirit to release their miracles. Everything from the music to the testimonies were choreographed to precision for pristine faith. Over several decades, millions of people came to the healing campaigns expecting miracles, because these men knew something about creating faith in the atmosphere. If you have seen pictures or videos of these great faith events, perhaps you have seen the wheelchairs and crutches stacked in piles at the altars. In fact, for evangelist Raymond T. Richey it wasn't uncommon for there to be several piles of discarded crutches left behind after his healing nights. After services he would put a match to them and make a bonfire for the Lord. People's faith was ignited!

Jesus, the Original Healing Evangelist

Jesus had the same quality; He was the original healing Evangelist! He had the gift of changing the atmosphere. Jesus would walk into a room, a city, or along the seashore where people would burst with faith because miracles were about to happen. There was such a strong faith and expectation of miracles that complete villages were healed.

> *And his fame went throughout **all** Syria: and they brought unto him **all** sick people that were taken with divers diseases and torments, and those which were possessed with devils, and those which were lunatick, and those that had the palsy; and he **healed them**.*   (Matthew 4:24)

Jesus ignited faith in those around Him. Jesus was so radiant with faith that when He walked into a city, people would crowd around Him in the streets to watch His every movement. They would travel from all over the country to see Him. They knew that He could work miracles. There was a buzz, or an electricity, in the cities where Jesus ministered.

> *And he came down with **them**, and stood in the plain, and the company of his disciples, and a great multitude of people out of **all** Judaea and Jerusalem, and from the sea*

*coast of Tyre and Sidon, which came to hear him, and to be **healed** of their diseases.* (Luke 6:17)

One thing was needed to see a miracle from Jesus—faith! Faith is needed to release miracles in people's lives.

*Then touched he their eyes, saying, **According to your faith** be it unto you.* (Matthew 9:29)

Jesus didn't find faith in every atmosphere He preached. When this happened, He would either do something to change it or He would walk away from it without doing miracles.

And when Jesus came into the ruler's house, and saw the minstrels and the people making a noise, he said unto them, Give place: for the maid is not dead, but sleepeth. And they laughed him to scorn. But when the people were put forth, he went in, and took her by the hand, and the maid arose. And the fame hereof went abroad into all that land. (Matthew 9:23–26)

When Jesus needed to pray for someone, He had to move the doubters out of the room. He knew that He had to remove the natural thinking of death, failure, and fear out of the air so that He could bring the supernatural thinking of life, victory, and faith into the air. When unbelievers mocked or scorned the crazy idea that a little girl could be raised from the dead, Jesus

> ALL HEALING AND MIRACLE NIGHTS DEPEND ON AN ATMOSPHERE OF FAITH; IF THIS IS NOT PRESENT, THEY WILL NOT BE SUCCESSFUL.

commanded them to leave the room. Then He had a room full of only believers who wanted to see the child come back to them. Faith could now be ignited because there were no hindrances. All healing and miracle nights depend on an atmosphere of faith; if this is not present, they will not be successful.

One night in the small town of Badapada, which is in the dangerous state of Odisha, there were five hundred people present at a church I was about to preach in. These people were already charged in faith by the time I had come to preach. I spoke about why Jesus had 100 percent miracle-working power that left cities completely healed. The place was so crowded that there was no place for me to move around to pray for the sick. We couldn't have them gather in the prayer lines as we usually did in India services. In fact, when I tried to go into the crowd, a stampede almost crushed me. My translator looked at me and told me to pray a quick prayer, then we could go back to our hotel. And yet, I felt that all these people needed me to lay hands on them. So, I was in a spot that I needed to hear from God on what to do. My spirit was moved to do something different. I felt inspired by the Holy Spirit to climb out the window of the church. I took two translators with me to the front doors of the church. Then I sent one translator back to the platform with instructions to ask everyone to start exiting the building in single file. I prayed for them as they left the building. When we got the room down to around two hundred people, we closed the doors and prayed for them in prayer lines. I left that village excited about the miracles that had occurred that night.

A few weeks after I got home to the US, I received a call from my friend Johnny, who told me of something special that had happened the night we visited his hometown, Badapada. His sister had told him that many testimonies of healings and miracles had come from all over the city. Everyone in attendance that night had been healed and had received their

> WHEN FAITH IS STIRRED WITHIN YOU, ANYTHING CAN HAPPEN—WHEREVER, WHATEVER, AND WHOEVER YOU ARE! UNBELIEF, DOUBT, AND FEAR MAKE IT HARD TO DO MIRACLES.

miracles. That means that there had been five hundred people healed and five hundred miracles released! But then he told me something else. He said that when they had walked through the villages after I had left, they had found no more sick people among them—neither Hindu, Muslim, nor Christian. They'd counted an additional five hundred people who had been healed who hadn't even attended the service. *How were they healed?* I wondered to myself. *How did they get faith?* Then I remembered something that I had noticed around the church building and its fences. They had the place wired with speakers that had broadcasted the message across the whole city. When I'd preached my sermon, it had been broadcasted and translated to the entire city. Those who were working in the market, resting at home, and walking the streets had heard the Word of God. Faith cometh by hearing!

So then faith cometh by hearing, and hearing by the word of God. (Romans 10:17)

The atmosphere in Badapada was changed from fear and doubt to faith and victory. Faith ignited the entire city, releasing miracles and healing everyone! When faith is stirred within you, anything can happen—wherever, whatever, and whoever you are! Unbelief, doubt, and fear make it hard to do miracles. These three things are faith-stoppers. They are the opposite of faith and belief. Once Jesus ran into a situation where the people reasoned among themselves not to believe.

> *And his sisters, are they not all with us? Whence then hath this man all these things? And they were offended in him. But Jesus said unto them, A prophet is not without honour, save in his own country, and in his own house. And he did not many mighty works there because of their unbelief.* (Matthew 13:56–58)

Jesus, the original healing Evangelist, did not change the unbelief in the air and in the heart of these men. These people were not filled with faith like everyone else throughout the region. This shows us the power of doubt in a person's life. These people undoubtedly heard all the stories, testimonies, and hype of Jesus; yet they reasoned among themselves that this Guy was not as powerful as people said He was. They knew Him and His family. If there was something special about Him, they would have known it already. This Guy was not *the* guy.

THE PEOPLE WHO WOULDN'T BELIEVE MISSED OUT ON MIRACLES. HOW DID JESUS RESPOND? HE MOVED ON. HE DID NOT SIT THERE AND WAIT ON SOMEONE TO BELIEVE.

Let me tell you that the devil has been whispering the same thing into people's ears from the very beginning; but he is wrong! Jesus *is* the Guy! He is the One who does miracles. The people who wouldn't believe missed out on miracles. How did Jesus respond? He moved on. He did not sit there and wait on someone to believe. Faith requires the action of choosing to believe in Him. He performed a few miracles, then He just left. He was not going to waste time with those who did not believe. He didn't worry about it or feel sad about it. He didn't try to explain it or feel like it was His fault. He just walked away.

It is difficult to preach the gospel in a place where there is no faith. Countless times, I have preached in the US, Africa, and India, where there was no faith in the room. Despite my best attempts to change the atmosphere, there were few miracles. I remember some members of my team looking at me and wondering what had happened. Even when I preached at churches in the US, I could feel doubt in the air.

There is nothing you can do when people don't believe; you can preach and pray for them, but then you must leave. It's not your fault. There is nothing to explain. You aren't to blame. You just have to be faithful to your call and obey the Spirit. Preach the Word; then let it work for you. That is all you can do.

I love this Scripture. It provides understanding on why this happens in those situations:

> For unto us was the gospel preached, as well as unto them: but the word preached did not profit them, not being mixed with faith in them that heard it.   (Hebrews 4:2)

I had an experience in India similar to what had happened to Jesus in His hometown. I, too, was asked by the church leader to leave. I had been at a church in India that was deep in a mountain area. There had to have been hundreds of people gathered there for healings and miracles who had waited so long for us to show up that night. Many had been sick, and we had been so excited about the service. The whole city had been wired with speakers so that everyone could hear the service. Pastor Jorge had preached a wonderful sermon that night, and so faith had been stirring in the air. I had gone up to the podium to lead the miracle part of the service as I usually did. But, the minute I had taken the microphone to talk about miracles, the pastor of the church had stopped me. I had looked back at him to see what the issue had been and if he understood what I was doing. My translator and coordinator had told me that the pastor would not permit us to pray for the sick but only to pray a blessing over them and then close the service.

I looked out at the crowd of people, and I could actually see their faith for miracles. The pastor would not allow us to pray for healings and miracles in his church. This was really frustrating; so before losing my cool, I asked Pastor Jorge to handle it as I got my bags to leave. Jorge told the pastor that we would honor his request because we were in his church but that the pastor would have to answer to God for what he'd stopped tonight. After Jorge prayed to close the service and dismissed everyone, the other American ministers and I grabbed our bags and headed to the door. Our driver went to get the jeep and back it up for us. As we pushed through the crowd, people kept reaching to touch us to get us to pray for them. The minute they touched us, they were healed!

In India, the custom is to take off your shoes while in a church. So as we made it out of the church, we had to take a few minutes to put our shoes back on. My friends wanted to keep praying for the people as we did so. I told them we needed to get into the jeep because a greater crowd would be coming and it could be unsafe. So we made it into the jeep, but the windows were down. Within seconds, hands crammed into the opened windows. The only way to clear them out was to lay hands upon them and pray for them. As we touched people's hands, they stepped back from the jeep and cried, out loud, that they had been healed. In fact, some people who ran next to the jeep and touched the closed windows were healed. God is amazing! Miracles are released even when the enemy tries to stop them! Miracles can't be stopped by the devil if you believe!

Faith in the atmosphere is necessary for miracles!

CHAPTER 2

HOW TO IGNITE FAITH

Have you ever wondered why some people in large healing services get healed and others don't?

I remember attending healing services in the 1990s held at Long Beach Convention and Entertainment Center in Long Beach, California. I was a young Navy sailor stationed at the old Long Beach Naval Complex. Every time any ministry was holding a healing service at the convention center, I would get a personal leave from the ship to attend. I wanted to be around the atmosphere of faith. I didn't need healing for myself, but I wanted to be around the healings and the presence of God. I knew that if healings were happening, the presence of God was there.

I remember when I saw God's glory fall on a man who was standing just behind where I was seated. He seemed to be feeling God's presence, but something was hindering him from receiving his miracle. I had been in and around the healing ministry long enough to know that someone needed to lay hands on him. So, a young healing minister myself, I laid my hands on him. Immediately, he fell to the ground in the Spirit, then got up and yelled that he had been healed. Afterward, people began to crowd around me and ask me to pray for them. The ushers immediately stopped me and politely told me that I wasn't allowed to pray for others during the service. Puzzled, I honored their request and didn't pray for anyone. I stayed for the rest of the service but could not help but notice the crowd that had approached me for prayer. Their hands were lifted, and they were crying out to God, asking Him to release their miracle.

When the service ended, those people left still hoping for their miracle. Later that night back in my hotel room, my heart struggled with the image of those people walking out of the arena with no healings or miracles. Those people loved God and looked like they truly believed that He would heal them. But at the end of the night, they walked away disappointed. Why?

I tried to understand why the ushers had stopped me from praying. The only thing I could think is that it was not my event. Period. I was not the man that God was using that hour. The Word of God says,

Let all things be done decently and in order.
(1 Corinthians 14:40)

There is an order in which all gifts need to operate. Understanding this was very important. God has a right way in which we are to conduct ministry. He sends His servants to specific areas to reach those He has drawn through the Holy Spirit. These servants have a God-given authority in the

Spirit. If it's their event, they have the authority to instruct, coordinate, and dictate how things will go. Most likely, they have prayed for it and raised the funds for it, and they must run the event. God's hand is on them, and anyone who works with them must work under their authority.

Take Control of Your Event

That simple understanding gave me some deep insight into how to operate with others in ministry for years to come. In fact, I had the same thing occur in one of my healing services the first year I was in India. There was a young Indian minister who kind of jumped the gun when we started to prepare for the healing service. I was concerned because the area where we were ministering had never before seen the power of God move. I had the responsibility of pastoring the movement and keeping the people from fearing what God was doing due to lack of understanding. But this young man had been known to interrupt services, doing this with a group of other people, as well. So, I kindly sent a few people back to ask him to stop and to please join us in the prayer line. He refused and kept going.

I have never been shy when it comes to telling anyone anything, especially when it comes to the gospel. So I went over to where he was standing and again asked him to kindly join us in the prayer line as my guest. Very nicely and politely, he refused again. The people were still praising God as we prepared for the prayer part of the service. Now, I am six foot tall and over 220 pounds, so I am naturally built like a NFL football player. I gently grabbed his arms and pulled them together. Smiling, I looked in his eyes and told him to show me that he was a man who could submit to authority. I told him that he could willingly come sit down with us in the front or that I would personally escort him from the tent. He and his men immediately left the meeting, saying that they had other places to which God was sending them.

Till this day, five years after our first meeting in India, I still see this guy pop up at my events. When I approach him to talk, he runs off.

Remember, if God sends you somewhere to do His work, you have to take control of your event. Just a note to the zealous ministers out there: You must submit yourselves to other ministers in brotherly love. If you are visiting another minister's event, you must be obedient to his authority.

Leaders Are Responsible for the Faith in the Atmosphere

As a man or woman of God chosen for a specific work, you are ultimately responsible for the faith in that atmosphere. Healings, miracles, and answered prayers all hinge not only on raising people's faith but also maintaining a high level of faith in the atmosphere.

> HEALINGS, MIRACLES, AND ANSWERED PRAYERS ALL HINGE NOT ONLY ON RAISING PEOPLE'S FAITH BUT ALSO MAINTAINING A HIGH LEVEL OF FAITH IN THE ATMOSPHERE.

I grew up attending tent revivals, healing crusades, and every faith ministry that would come to the old Sam Houston Coliseum in Houston, Texas. I have seen great men of God, such as Morris Cerullo, R. W. Schambach and

Oral Roberts, operate in strong atmospheres of faith. In these events, it was so important to keep a high level of faith to release miracles. Any interruptions or unplanned movement could deflate the faith level in a room.

I remember growing up in my teens as a member of Lakewood Church in Houston, Texas. My pastor, John Osteen, used to tell people to stop moving around during his altar calls. Any movement could interrupt what God was trying to do for someone, and could be a distraction to someone who needed a touch from God. I have heard this same instruction echoed from other great healing ministers, evangelists, and pastors throughout the years. This tells me that receiving miracles is dependent on the amount of faith in the atmosphere—high levels of faith make miracles happen, while low levels of faith make miracles difficult.

Why People Don't Get Miracles

Still thinking about those people who wanted me to pray for them, I began to dissect the night. One thing I noticed was that those people who crowded around me for prayer never got to go up onstage for prayer. Because there are usually thousands of people who attend healing events at stadiums, convention centers, and arenas, the amount of people who actually get to go onstage is very limited. And there is something that happens to a person's faith level when a man of God lays hands on him—faith ignites!

Now, in typical services like these, after the preaching and worship, there is usually a time of prayer for specific individuals lead by the leader. Many of the people in these conferences get their miracles during this moment. Their faith ignites and releases their miracle. But not everyone receives his or her miracle. Many are like the people who came up to me and left disappointed. There is a moment when a person's faith releases his or her miracle. For many, this release happens when a man of God personally prays for them.

For example, the only person around me that night who was excited about getting healed was the man whom I had laid hands on. There is a moment when faith boils over and is ready to ignite. That man was ready to get his miracle the very second I laid hands on him. The air had been stirred for a miracle. The man tapped into the atmosphere. All I did was ignite the faith he already had to release his miracle.

God Wants Your Faith, Not Your Fear

The second thing I noticed was that some of the people looked worried that they wouldn't get their miracles that night. God wants your faith, not your fear. If a person is desperate or anxious, fear will take over him or her. Fear is the opposite of faith.

> GOD WANTS YOUR FAITH, NOT YOUR FEAR. IF A PERSON IS DESPERATE OR ANXIOUS, FEAR WILL TAKE OVER HIM OR HER. FEAR IS THE OPPOSITE OF FAITH.

During one of my first nights ministering in India, a great amount of fear and anxiousness took over the service. Over a million Hindus had gathered for Holi, also known as the festival of colors, directly across from my small tent of three hundred people. The attendees were so afraid that, no matter what I did, I could not encourage them to believe for a miracle.

That night, I prayed to God that He would help me remove this spirit of fear from my conference. In the middle of the night, Jesus came into my room and sat on the edge of my bed. I didn't see Him but felt Him there. He said to preach on His name. So, the following night, I preached on all the names of God that I could remember. The Hindu crowd was getting restless outside our tent. When I got to the last name, I commanded that the demons, fallen angels, evil spirits, and the devil know Jesus by the Ancient of Days! The heavens opened directly above our tent, and we felt a wind blow down from every corner. The noise of the millions of Hindus faded. We looked outside, and everyone was gone! I believe God sent His angels to force them all away. Our healing ministry in India was never the same after that event. We have seen the number of miracles grow every year we have returned. This was also a breakthrough for me personally to have confidence that He had called me to do what He had told me to do. You must have confidence that you can do whatever God has called you to do. You must be willing and able to answer any call in faith that He sends into your life, not only because you believe, but also because you are called by Him. Confidence will build the faith required to complete the task at hand.

Stay Focused on God, Not on Your Sickness or Need

In my healing services in the US, I often find myself telling the individuals I pray for to stay focused on God. I tell them not to think of their sickness or need but to fellowship with God, because He wants to spend time with them and bless them. I have seen that, as they relax, God heals them.

One lady in my healing service was from Humble, Texas. She had broken her hand two years before and had never gotten it reset, and she didn't have the money to pay for the surgery to fix it. She couldn't bend it or lift it above her shoulders. When I approached her to pray, she explained her injury to me. She seemed so anxious and nervous. Softly I asked her to just think on the Lord and not on her injury. I told her that God knew her need and wanted to spend time with her, and that all she needed to do was talk to Him and receive His love. She calmed down and cried softly. The whole time I had been talking to her, I'd slowly massaged and bended her arm. Then I moved it completely above her shoulder and asked if her arm had been healed. She opened her eyes and cried out that God had healed her broken arm!

Miracles happen when we think on God, not on our problems!

CHAPTER 3

DELAYED MIRACLES

Ignited Faith Delivers Delayed Miracles

Many times I have heard testimonies of people who have left my services sick but are healed later. Some people were healed the same day, while others were healed the next day or even weeks later.

Faith believes in something that is unseen. Faith knows that everything is possible. The Bible says,

> Now faith is the substance of things hoped for, the evidence of things not seen. (Hebrews 11:1)

We must understand that faith takes time to manifest results. Let's take a look at an example. When you sow a financial seed, it takes time for that seed to grow. You can't give an offering or a gift and then expect your finances to immediately be fixed. You have to give your seeds time to grow into what you need.

I sowed a monthly seed to a local Christian radio station in Houston for a year. The whole time I sowed, I believed that one day I would have my own radio station for the Lord. Four years later, I started my own online radio station, RevMedia Network. It took time for those seeds to produce in the natural what my faith believed in the supernatural.

Do the same principles of faith and time apply to healings? Yes; I have seen thousands of people instantly and miraculously healed; but I have also seen hundreds of people leave my events and get their miracle another day.

When I was a young man of God, I visited a church where my future brother-in-law belonged. His pastor preached that night, and at the end of the service, he asked all the young preachers to come up to the altar. There were about five ministers, including myself, who were lined up in front at the altar. Then he asked those who were sick or needed a touch from the Lord to come forward so that one of these ministers could pray for them. I didn't know anyone there besides my future brother-in-law and my sister, so my line was empty. All the other ministers' lines were long. I stood in the corner and patiently waited for someone to pray for. Then, all of sudden, a very short lady walked up to me for prayer. I told her that I was glad she'd come to my line. She said that she didn't really have a choice, because all the other lines were too long and she needed to work in the morning. So I was chosen by default. I asked her for her prayer request, and she said it was unspoken. So I prayed a short prayer for her. Basically, I just asked the Lord, who knew her needs, to meet them tonight. "Lord," I pleaded, "heal her body in Jesus' name, amen."

She looked at me and asked, "That's it?"

"Yep," I told her.

"Oh, well, okay I guess." She looked at the other lines and then said, "I guess I am going home. Thanks."

Three months later, at my sister's wedding reception, someone jumped on my back. I turned around to see who it was, and to my surprise, it was the short young woman whom I had prayed for at my brother-in-law's church that night. She asked if I remembered her and then said, "I have to tell you a story of what happened after you had prayed for me. All my life, I had to get out of my bed on my knees and crawl to my bathroom to get ready in the morning. My feet were curled ever since I was a child, and I needed special shoes just to get ready every day. So, after going to the bathroom, I would go to my closet to put on special shoes that I had to wear in order to walk. This was an embarrassing issue I had never spoken about to anyone.

"When you prayed for me, I really thought that it wasn't much of a prayer. But I believed what you had said about my healing, and told the Lord that I believed what you had prayed over me and that I received my healing. The next morning, I woke up to get ready for my day. As I stood in my bathroom washing my face, I stared into the mirror. Then I started to cry, because I'd noticed that, for the first time in my life, I had stepped out of my bed, put my feet on the ground, and walked to the bathroom. Amen! My feet were no longer curled; they were healed!"

The first thing this woman did before telling anyone was go and buy shoes. Yes, miracles can take a day! They can be there waiting for you a day or week or month later. Your miracle will be released!

Ignited Faith Releases Miracles That Will Manifest in Time

I ministered in Odisha, India, a few years back, and the whole trip, I saw miracles manifesting everywhere. On this particular trip, we had a breakthrough in our healing ministry in India. I was preaching at the last church on my trip before heading back to the airport. After I preached, I asked if there was anyone who needed prayer for healing. A few people in the back of the church waved to me, where I saw a little old lady lying in a bed. They told me that she had been crippled since birth. I thought to myself, *Great—they brought me the hardest case first.* I prayed for her and told her that, in one week, she would feel her legs; in two weeks, she would be able to stand; and in three weeks, she would walk into this church and would testify of the goodness of God.

Three weeks later, I was back home in my office when I got an e-mail, a text, and a phone call from three different people. They all confirmed that the woman whom I had prayed for had come to the church to testify of her healing exactly how I'd said it would happen. Sometimes, miracles take days, months, and even

> IT DOESN'T MATTER IF THE MIRACLE YOU PRAY FOR COMES THE DAY YOU PRAY FOR IT; IT HAS BEEN RELEASED AND IS ON ITS WAY. THE MOMENT FAITH IGNITES, A MIRACLE IS RELEASED.

years to manifest. God is good! In this situation, faith was ignited, and the woman walked it out. It doesn't matter if the miracle you pray for comes the day you pray for it; it has been released and is on its way. The moment faith ignites, a miracle is released. The enemy will fight up until the moment you get it!

The Devil Cannot Take What Your Faith Has Released

Look at Daniel's experience with a delayed answer in his life:

> *Then said he ["a certain man clothed in linen" (verse 5)] unto me, Fear not, Daniel: for from the first day that thou didst set thine heart to understand, and to chasten thyself before thy God, thy words were heard, and I am come for thy words. But the prince of the kingdom of Persia withstood me one and twenty days: but, lo, Michael, one of the chief princes, came to help me; and I remained there with the kings of Persia.* (Daniel 10:12–13)

When Daniel prayed to the Lord, his answer was not sent out immediately. He waited twenty-one days until he received a natural manifestation. But it had been sent to him the moment his faith had ignited. The devil and his fallen angels had actually fought the angel who was delivering the miracle to Daniel.

First, for those who are wondering right now, let me tell you this: The devil cannot stop an angel of God from delivering a miracle of faith. It seems that he can delay it but not stop it. No matter how long the angel had to fight to deliver the miracle to Daniel, he eventually got through. We must believe!

Second, the angel did not lose the answer or blessing. Though the enemy delayed him, he couldn't take the blessing. Your blessing can't be stolen once your faith has released it. The devil can't take what your faith has released! You should shout with joy just hearing that message!

> YOUR BLESSING CAN'T BE STOLEN ONCE YOUR FAITH HAS RELEASED IT. THE DEVIL CAN'T TAKE WHAT YOUR FAITH HAS RELEASED!

Third, the devil's forces cannot stand against God's authority. God's promises will be delivered! It doesn't matter how many of the enemy's forces delay your miracle; God's authority will eventually take over. The devil can't stop God!

When I pray for people in India, they usually separate into lines of men, women, and children. I basically lay my hands on each of them for five seconds as I walk down the line; then I make my way back to the front. Sometimes, the kids actually run in front of me as I quickly lay my hands on them. It tends to be like that game Whac-A-Mole at kids' eateries. The gopher jumps out of the hole, and you must quickly hit it back down again. As the children go by me, it is hard to even ask them what they need, let alone pray for them to receive a miracle by faith.

Let me tell you of a little boy who lives in the mountains and jungles of the Gajapati District in Odisha, India. He suffered with crooked legs all his life. This little boy was in one of those prayer lines for kids and went by me as quickly as the other kids, so I was not able to spend more than a few seconds praying for him. Two hours after that healing service, I went on to my next service in the evening.

Later I found out that the little boy was working with his father eighty kilometers away from where I had prayed for him. As he walked up a set of stairs, he marveled and called his mother on the cell phone. She heard him crying on the other line and asked if he had fallen down again. He said, "No, Momma, I feel Jesus touching my legs." As he walked up the steps, God started to heal the boy's legs! As he stood on top of the staircase, he cried out, "I am healed! I am healed! Jesus has healed my legs, making them straight!" He and his mother cried and glorified God. Amen! Miracles happen even when there is a delay.

When Your Faith Ignites the Release, Miracles Happen Even Though Delayed

You would think that healing ministers have all the faith they need for healings. They have seen all these miracles with their own eyes. Surely they can find the faith to heal themselves. The truth is that, twice, I have had pain in my gluteus maximus muscle so unbearable that I sought God to heal me because I did not want to stop traveling to preach the gospel. It was harsh and uncomfortable, and it troubled me as I flew around the world, because I could not sit down for long periods of time. A nineteen-hour plane ride was torture. I would take Ibuprofen and just pray that I would get through it.

For almost ten months, I could feel the pain all day as I worked in my office and traveled. Just driving my car on short trips was uncomfortable. I had to change my workouts and stop running; walking was the best I could do. I prayed for many people during those ten months; yet every night I came home, I was still in pain. But I believed every day that I would get healed. Eventually, my faith ignited and released a manifestation. After ten months, I woke up in the morning, and the pain was gone for good.

Shortly after that healing, I helped my brother lift a 300-pound safe into his pickup truck. The safe slipped and almost crushed him. I positioned myself to lift it higher so that he could clear himself, and, eventually, we got the safe into the truck. That day, my left knee felt okay; but in the morning, I couldn't walk much on it. Over the next five months, I tried not to limp as I took planes around the country, went on mission trips, held healing services, and visited TV stations. But my knee hurt so badly that I thought my leg would just fall off. I had faith but no healing. I saw many miracles in my services during those five months, including blind eyes opened and backs healed. In fact, one night in Lafayette, Louisiana, there was an amazing healing of knees. Everyone with a knee problem was healed in that service; we actually heard bones popping. One lady was healed as I preached. I prayed for one lady whose knee had been hurting for seven years, making her unable to play with her grandchildren, and she fell out in the Spirit. When she got up, she was healed!

That night, when I saw these healings, I thought that surely it was my night to be healed. But nothing happened; the pain was still there. Later I found out that I had torn my ACL. I thought that I would need to go get surgery because the last five months of knee pain had been even harder than the ten months I had suffered with the rear-end pain.

In December, I limped onto the plane to Africa. By that time, my injury was very noticeable; yet I still went on the trip. On the fourth to last night of the trip, I was preaching during my healing service when I felt a twitch in my knee. The pain was still there but wasn't as strong. Each day after that, my knee felt better and better. On the last morning, I went onstage to preach in full assurance that there was no more pain in my knee. I preached like a younger version of myself, having fun with the crowd and testifying to them I was healed. I jumped up and down onstage, which was something I couldn't do for months. Then I jumped off the stage, which I probably shouldn't have done. Oh, thank God for His grace when we do something crazy. God healed me when my faith ignited; even though there was a delay, it did not stop the blessing from being released! Praise God.

Though it may take time for it to reach us,
a miracle has been released!

CHAPTER 4

WHOSOEVER, WHATSOEVER MIRACLES

"Whosoever" Can Have "Whatsover" Miracle If He Believes

In Mark 11, Jesus cursed a fig tree that was not producing fruit. The fig tree did not immediately die or wither away in front of the disciples' eyes. But on the way back from their journey, they passed the fig tree and were amazed that it had withered away and was dead. Jesus must have been frustrated with them because they couldn't grasp such a simple principle. The Bible says,

> And Jesus answering saith unto them, **Have faith in God.** For verily I say unto you, That **whosoever** shall say unto this **mountain,** Be thou removed, and be thou cast into the sea; and shall not doubt in his heart, but shall believe that those things which he saith shall come to pass; he shall have **whatsoever** he saith.   (Mark 11:22–23)

"*Whosoever*" is me and you. "*Whatsover*" is our need or miracle. Jesus said that the main component we need to activate this Scripture in our lives is to have faith in God. Having faith in God alone releases His will in our lives for miracles. This principle seems very simple: Just believe that you will receive what you ask for, and it shall happen; but it isn't simple. The disciples seemed amazed that the plant had withered—almost more amazed than they were at any other miracle Jesus performed. This was one of the only miracles they seemed excited about, and they specifically pointed it out to Jesus. Why were they so excited about this particular miracle? There are several things I want to point out.

> WORDS AND BELIEF RELEASE OUR MIRACLES! THE VERY WORDS JESUS SPOKE TO THE FIG TREE WERE SPOKEN WITH THE SAME AUTHORITY HE USED TO PERFORM OTHER MIRACLES.

First, it was one of the few miracles Jesus performed that did not bring something back to life or produce something. In fact, it could have been easily been a story in which Jesus commanded figs to grow. But instead, He told the tree to wither and die. It was done exactly how Jesus had commanded. Not long after Jesus had cursed the tree, it died. In this example, Jesus showed us how powerful our words are. Words and belief release our miracles! The very words Jesus spoke to the fig tree were spoken with the same authority He used to perform other miracles. For example, He commanded the wind and the sea to calm down with the same authority; He commanded demons and sicknesses to leave with the same authority. He knew that if

He asked for anything and believed unwaveringly, it would be done. We read in Isaiah,

> So shall my word be that goeth forth out of my mouth: it shall not **return** unto me **void**, but it shall accomplish that which I please, and it shall prosper in the thing whereto I sent it. (Isaiah 55:11)

Jesus demonstrated this Scripture in the fig tree story so that we would know that our words are powerful when we believe.

Pray and Believe Until Your Miracle Is Released

When I was on a mission trip visiting Serve International Ministries in Kakamega, Kenya, I saw something amazing that really inspired me. The weather had been clear most of the week, but right at the beginning of a conference, it began raining hard. If the conference was being held in a normal-sized building in the US, rain wouldn't matter as much. But the roof of the building we were in was made out of thin tin sheets, and the sound of the rain hitting the tin would have drown out the guest speaker's voice.

So, before he started, the president of Serve International Ministries, Paul Ligono, took the microphone from the singers onstage. Paul is a short, thin Kenyan man, but he has great faith! He told the crowd that today was not going to be a rainy day. He said that he recognized that it was an attack of the enemy, and that he refused to give him any glory by allowing him to disrupt our service with rain. He said that God was stronger and more powerful than the enemy, and that we all needed to believe. Then he began to lead us in a prayer against the rain. For the next thirty minutes, this man prayed against the storm by rebuking the wind, the rain, and the clouds. He commanded it when to go, where to go, and when to come back. He went on to say that rain was good in Kenya, a blessing because it brings life, but not over the meetinghouse this week.

Jesus demonstrated the exact same control over the environment many times during His miracle ministry. His words took dominion over the atmosphere and created faith. We read in the Bible that, when Jesus cast demons out of a boy, the demons requested to be sent into the pigs.

> *And [Jesus] asked [the demon], What is thy name? And he answered, saying, My name is Legion: for we are many. And he besought him much that he would not send them away out of the country. Now there was there nigh unto the mountains a great herd of swine feeding. And all the devils besought him, saying, Send us into the swine, that we may enter into them. And forthwith Jesus gave them leave. And the unclean spirits went out, and entered into the swine: and the herd ran violently down a steep place into the sea, (they were about two thousand;) and were choked in the sea.*   (Mark 5:9–13)

How long would you have prayed for the rain to stop? Would you have given it ten minutes before giving up? I saw a Kenyan man pray until the rain stopped. He stood onstage and yelled, danced, and prayed until it stopped. Then, at the end of the conference, it resumed. Amazing! I saw and heard a faith that was so powerful, it stopped the rain!

My Whosoever, Whatsoever Moments on the Airplane

I preached the "whosoever, whatsoever" message in several healing services during the fall. By the time I preached it in Kenya during the Christmas holiday, it was deep within my spirit. Something truly special happened there—my knee was healed. Now I could finally walk through the airport without pain in my knee.

On my way home, when I had to catch a connecting flight at Schiphol International Airport in Amsterdam, I recognized the agent at the security gate from my previous stopovers. Smiling, I told her that it was good to see her again. She looked at me surprised that I had noticed her and apologized the she did not remember me. I told her that it was fine, because she had seen too many people to remember me, but that every time I saw her, she was a blessing. She scanned my ticket and read my name out loud. "David Yanez. I won't forget it."

After boarding the plane and finding my seat in economy comfort section, I noticed it was a very crowded flight. While sitting there, I looked directly in front of me at all the room in first class. That is the moment when my spirit took over for a "whosoever, whatsoever miracle." Unknowingly, I began praying out loud, saying that I was *whosoever* and that I could have *whatsoever* I believed. I prayed and believed that, before the attendants closed the airplane doors, I would be upgraded to business class for free. Everyone in the economy comfort section laughed at me, but I just smiled, because I didn't even realize I was praying out loud.

Almost immediately after praying, a lady started complaining to me that I was sitting in her seat. My seat and ticket matched, so I didn't budge. Within five minutes of that prayer, the KLM airline gate agent that I had thanked earlier came in calling my name. "David Yanez, is she telling you that you are in her seat?"

I turned around and noticed that it was my new KLM friend. "I am glad you're here," I said. "Yes, she is complaining about the seat assignment."

"It is her seat now," she responded, "because you have been upgraded to business class for free. Grab your bags!"

The whole section of the plane was silent. I stood up with my bags and said, "God answers prayers!" As I sat there in business class watching the gate walkway retract, I couldn't help but be awed and humbled—awed at the quick response to my prayer and humbled by a simple request being granted. This also showed me that appreciating a person's everyday job may mean a lot to him or her. Also, sushi, steak, unlimited Coke in a chilled glass, real silverware, and a reclining seat that feels like a custom La-Z-Boy recliner are blessings, too. Thank you, Lord, for small blessings after a long journey. God surely knows how to bless. My Bible says that we are blessed going in and blessed going out. (See Deuteronomy 28:6.) Amen!

Speaking to Clouds

Recently, I preached the whosoever, whatsoever message at a three-night healing service at a church in Louisville, Kentucky. After, in my hotel room, I got my bags ready to check out. It was around 11:15 AM, and the pastor of the church was on his way to pick me up for lunch, then to take me to the airport to catch my 4 PM flight back to Houston. But I received a text on my phone from the airlines warning me that my connecting flight from Atlanta to Houston had been cancelled due to a bad forecast of winter storms.

Immediately, I called the airlines' help desk to arrange another flight. An attendant told me that a winter storm had badly hit Houston the previous Friday, and that a similar storm was projected to hit that evening. The airports and entire city would be closed by 6 PM, and the airlines didn't expect to begin rebooking flights to Houston for two days. So, basically, I would be stuck in Louisville or Atlanta longer than expected. I asked the agent if she could get me on an earlier flight, but she told me no. I asked her to look one more time for a flight from Louisville to Atlanta leaving within the next hour. She told me surprisingly that she had just found a flight from Louisville to Atlanta in exactly one hour that would allow me to catch the last flight into Houston. She also said that only one seat remained on both flights and that I had to choose now what to do.

My pastor friend was not even going to be at the hotel to pick me up until just before 12 PM, so I needed a ride to the airport. Right at that moment, I heard a knock on my hotel room door. I looked outside to see who it could be. It was a man from the church I had just preached at over the weekend. I opened the door, and the man asked me if it was okay for him to visit for a few minutes for a brief prayer. The first thing I asked him was if he knew how to get to the airport and how far away it was. He said that he worked there and that it was only fifteen minutes away.

So I told the agent over the phone to book the ticket. She said that my tickets would be ready by the time that I got there, but that, because she did not have a confirmation number, I would have to find someone there to issue me the tickets.

I looked at my new friend and told him to grab my bags and that we would pray on the way to the airport. I dropped off the room keys at the front desk to check out, then we left. When I made it to the airport, I went through security and found my gate. As I was in the air heading to Atlanta, I spoke to the storm and commanded it to completely miss Houston. I told it to pass Houston and to hit New Orleans, then to go as far as Atlanta. I believed that I was whosoever and that I could have whatsoever, as long as I believed.

After landing, I kept on praying and watching the flight board to make sure my flight to Houston had not been cancelled. Finally, I heard an announcement that it was time to board the flight and that it was the last one going there today. Dozens of people were standing there waiting for an available seat. In fact, I wondered if I had been bumped, because when I scanned my ticket to board, I heard a beep, which usually signifies a seat change or standby status. The gate agents gave me a new stub, then told me that I had been upgraded to first class. I just smiled because God knew how to surprise me. There I was, worrying about being bumped, when God had already gotten me not only the last seat on the plane but a first-class ticket.

While I stared at the clouds in the air, I smiled again, thinking that the clouds had been beaten. After landing at George Bush Intercontinental Airport and exiting the plane, I saw that many flights had been cancelled on the screens in the terminal.

My wife picked me up from the airport and told me that the kids were excited because they had gotten a snow day both today and tomorrow. I broke the news to her that there would be no snow today or tomorrow, because the storm was passing us and hitting New Orleans and Atlanta. That night and the following morning, my kids waited for snow, but it never came. The storm hit New Orleans and Atlanta! In fact, Atlanta had one of the worst winter storms in its history. My kids weren't pleased, but I was.

Words Can Either Create or Halt Miracles

In the same way that our words release miracles, they will also keep miracles from happening. Faith requires that there be no doubt, worries, or fear. Any one of these will suck faith out of any room like a vacuum. I have seen strong spiritual men and women of God lose all faith after being diagnosed with an illness. The Bible says,

> For his anger **endureth** but a moment; in his favour is life: **weeping** may endure for a night, but joy cometh in the morning. (Psalm 30:5)

Yes, emotions hit us, and, upon discovering bad news, we are sad and may cry. But there is a time when our faith needs to rise above our weeping to prepare for a miracle. Jesus Himself could do nothing without faith. He even cleared all doubters out of a house so that they would not affect the atmosphere of faith for healing. (See Matthew 9:23–26.)

There is a fine line between faith and fear. In order for faith or fear to produce results, we must believe in them. Positive words of encouragement and Scriptures will produce

IN ORDER FOR FAITH OR FEAR TO PRODUCE RESULTS, WE MUST BELIEVE IN THEM. POSITIVE WORDS OF ENCOURAGEMENT AND SCRIPTURES WILL PRODUCE FAITH IN US. NEGATIVE WORDS OF DISCOURAGEMENT AND LIES WILL PRODUCE FEAR.

faith in us. Negative words of discouragement and lies will produce fear. God's Word tells us that we are blessed and not cursed. (See Ephesians 1:3.) When a person gets a bad diagnosis or bad news, he needs to choose what he will believe—man's report or God's report. That reminds me of the popular song "Whose Report Shall You Believe." The chorus goes, "We shall believe the report of the Lord." God will always out-bless man in all ways. All people, at some time or another, have received bad reports. We must be careful in how we respond to them.

Many people who have attended my healing services are fearful, desperate, and have no hope. I went to Nairobi, Kenya, to visit a church where we had planned to have some meetings over the weekend. When we got there, we met with the pastor to make sure all the equipment was ready for the next morning's conference. As we were talking in the parking lot, the pastor's cousin, Joshua, walked into the complex. Joshua was happy to see us, but he began sharing sad news with us, saying that he was very sick with pneumonia. He had spent days trying to get an appointment, but the hospital had said he didn't have insurance and sent him to a clinic. The clinic had been closed until Monday, so he hadn't been able to get medicine or even to see a doctor this whole time. This guy kept going on for a while about his issues.

The pastor introduced us to Joshua as healing ministers, but not once did he ask us to pray for him. As we visited outside, he kept going back to discussing his pain. When we mentioned that we were headed to get some refreshments and snacks before going to the hotel, he said that he was too sick to join us. As the other men were getting into a car, I walked to where Joshua was standing. I grabbed him by the shoulders and looked into his eyes. I asked him if he believed that Jesus would heal him, and he said that he did! So I told him that I was going to pray for him and that God was going to heal him; and that, after I prayed for him, I didn't want to hear another word about how sick he was, how much pain he felt, or anything else about his sickness. He agreed with my terms.

So I prayed for him for just a few seconds. Then we got into the car and drove off to get a cold Coke together. During the drive, he didn't speak much at all. I assumed he thought he was in trouble. Honestly, sometimes it takes a direct confrontation to make someone aware of what he is doing. We sat at the restaurant drinking tea and Coke, laughing, and sharing stories. Not once during our fellowship did he mention his sickness or excuses.

After, while Joshua and I were watching soccer matches on TV across the room from each other, Joshua suddenly called out my name. "Dr. David, I am healed; I am healed!" He stood up, took a deep breath, bent down to touch his legs, and then bent to one side and then backward—all the things he previously couldn't do without pain. I went over to celebrate with him! When we speak positive words of faith, God honors our belief!

⌒

I had just finished holding a miracle night in India when I was asked to visit a pastor's sick wife in their home. Now, I never go to people's houses in India. This is a rule I had put in place because of the radical Hindus who are known to burn down Christian homes. But this particular moment, I felt that I should quickly go in to pray. The pastor's wife was paralyzed and had lain in bed for six months.

As I kneeled down to pray for her, she kept crying and telling me how it had just happened. Suddenly one morning, she had not been able to get out of bed. She did not know why it had happened to her. All she spoke about was what had happened since she had gotten sick.

I told her to stop talking about her sickness, because I was going to pray for her so that she would be healed, and that, after I prayed, she would be able to get out of bed and cook dinner for her husband. I prayed for her, then I left in my jeep and went back to the hotel. Before I arrived, we received a call from the pastor that his wife had gotten out of the bed and was cooking his favorite meal. He was very happy she had been healed but almost even happier about his favorite meal that she was cooking!

Stop talking negatively, and be healed!

CHAPTER 5

MIRACLES UNKNOWN

Sometimes, faith ignites even when you do not know you need a miracle. In one of my healing services in Nairobi, Kenya, a woman stood in my prayer line waiting for her turn. When I stood in front of her, I briefly laid hands on her. I told her that she was healed, then I went on to the next person in line.

After the service, she walked home with her friend who had invited her to the conference. She said to her that she didn't understand why the man of God had said that she was healed because she wasn't even sick.

Early the next morning, she called her friend to tell her some amazing news. She shared that, since she had been a child, she would wake up frozen in a fetal position, with her knees bent, for half an hour. During the morning, she would not be able to move even an inch until her body released from this position. She said that, after the night I had prayed for her, she had woken up and gotten out of bed immediately!

She was completely freed from whatever had been holding her body. She hadn't known she was sick the whole time! She testified how amazing it was that God could heal people even when they don't know they are sick. It does not matter if you know you have a sickness or not; when you hear the Word of God and believe, anything is possible.

The Spirit Knows What You Need

Now, how can the will of God be done in your life and how can you receive miracles you haven't asked for? How does God know what to do for you when you don't even ask? Don't we have to ask for a miracle for God to give us one? We read in Romans,

> For we know that the whole creation groaneth and travaileth in pain together until now. And not only they, but ourselves also, which have the firstfruits of the Spirit, even we ourselves groan within ourselves, waiting for the adoption, to wit, the redemption of our body. For we are saved by hope: but hope that is seen is not hope: for what a man seeth, why doth he yet hope for? But if we hope for that we see not, then do we with patience wait for it. Likewise the Spirit also helpeth our infirmities: for we know not what we should pray for as we ought: but the Spirit itself maketh intercession for us with groanings which cannot be uttered. And he that searcheth the hearts knoweth what is the mind of the Spirit, because he maketh intercession for the saints according to the will of God.
>
> (Romans 8:22–27)

The Spirit knows of your sickness within your physical body. The Word of God says in verse 26, "*For we know not what we should pray for as we ought.*" The Spirit Himself is interceding for your need even when you are unaware of it. God doesn't need you to know what you need because the Spirit of God knows. The Spirit of God does the will of God. What is the will of God for you? The Bible says,

> *Beloved, I wish above all things that thou mayest prosper and be in health, **even as thy soul** prospereth.*
>
> (3 John 1:2)

God wants you to be healthy, not just healed. What is the difference between being healthy and being healed? Being healthy means that your body is not hurt or aching. When you are healthy, it's not difficult to get out of bed in the morning and you don't dread the day because your body can't keep up with it. On the other hand, being healed means that your sickness is completely gone.

An old friend of mine who was a physician told me that our bodies were built to peak in health in our forties, then go downhill after that. There are more problems after age fifty because the body is dying. Those are horrible words, but they are true because of the curse that has been handed down to us after the fall in the garden of Eden. Each man is given a day and a time to die, or an expiration date. The Bible says in Ecclesiastes,

> *There is **no man that hath power over the spirit to retain the spirit;** neither hath he power in the day of death: and there is no discharge in that war.*
>
> (Ecclesiastes 8:8)

When God calls the spirit of a man home, there is no choice but for that man to die on that day, whether healthy or not. We will all die one day. But that doesn't mean it has to be today! It doesn't mean we have to be weak and broken in between life and death, either. We don't have to be sick in a hospital bed, sit in a wheelchair, or struggle financially until we die. God wants us to be healthy and blessed; the Bible is full of Scriptures that shout this truth to our spirits.

> *And Moses was an hundred and twenty years old when he died: his **eye** was **not dim**, nor his natural force abated.*
>
> (Deuteronomy 34:7)

> *For I will restore health unto thee, and I will heal thee of thy wounds, saith the* LORD*....*   (Jeremiah 30:17)

> *He sent his word, and healed them, and delivered them from their destructions.*   (Psalm 107:20)

> *Who his own self bare our sins in his own body on the tree, that we, being dead to sins, should live unto righteousness: by whose stripes ye were healed.*   (1 Peter 2:24)

A woman in the Mwiki slums on the outskirts of Nairobi, Kenya, had a huge burden one day. She had a small catering business in which she made food for parties and gatherings. A customer came by her place one day to place a huge order, which would financially change things for her and her two children. She was so excited to get the order, but she couldn't afford to purchase everything she needed to fulfill it. So, she borrowed money from friends and family members to complete the order. She even used the money she had set aside for rent and utilities for the month to finish the deal. When the order was completed, she notified the customer to pick it up. However, the customer never showed up, leaving her with the order and the debt.

She was devastated not only about the order but about losing her home. Depression fell on this woman so strongly. She called her sister to watch her kids and feed them a meal that night. She purposed in her heart to kill herself at a local soccer field. She took a kitchen knife, then started walking in the dark to the field. She told herself that she would kill herself by the goal post, so that the soccer players would find her body in the morning.

As she walked to the field, she was surprised to find my Mwiki Crusade. I was preaching a sermon the moment she had walked onto the field, and God told me to change the topic of my message to forgiveness. So I preached on how we must forgive, and said that forgiving was tied to our healing, finances, and blessings.

That night, I read from the book of Matthew:

Leave there thy gift before the altar, and go thy way; first be reconciled to thy brother, and then come and offer thy gift. (Matthew 5:24)

In the Word, Jesus tells us how important forgiveness is to God. He used a financial example to show us how our everyday lives are affected by unforgiveness.

As I preached on forgiveness at the Mwiki Crusade, I asked individuals who needed to forgive someone to come forward. The woman who had come to the field to kill herself decided to join the prayer line. As I prayed from the platform, my leaders went forward to pray for each person in the crowd.

Three days later, this woman came back to our Mwiki Crusade to testify of what God had done for her. She shared that while standing in that line that night, she had forgiven her father, family, and even the customer who hadn't picked up her order. That night, God had removed the spirit of suicide from her mind. She said that warmth had come into her heart and that she wanted to live! As she shared of all the things that had led to her suicide attempt, she cried and said that she wasn't worried about her situation because God was with her.

At that moment, I was led by the Lord to give her some money. I told my security guard to bring my bags to me, and I pulled out some money to hand to her. When the crowd saw what I was doing, everyone started running forward to bless her as if they were on the old game show *The Price Is Right*. We had a yellow five-gallon bucket that we placed onstage, and we took an offering for her that provided more than enough money for her to pay all her overdue bills and to pay back everyone she had borrowed from. She was given back all that the enemy had stolen from her—amen! The enemy has a plan for you, but God's plan is better.

> *The thief cometh not, but for to steal, and to kill, and to destroy: I am come that they might have life, and that they might have it more abundantly.*   (John 10:10)

Thank God the Spirit, who knows what you need before you do. Thank God the Spirit, who is praying inside you, groaning for your miracle. (See Romans 8:26.) Your miracle may be happening even when you don't know it!

God loves us so much that He intercedes for our needs we are unaware of!

CHAPTER 6

COMPASSION
MOVES GOD

Millions of people throughout the earth have benefitted from a divine supernatural release of miracles that God has freely given through His divine compassion. Compassion moves God to bestow miracles on us! We read in the Bible that Elisha was used by God to release miracles on two women. One of them was in financial crisis and the other needed a physical miracle. In both cases, God was moved by compassion to change their situations.

Compassion Moves God the Father to Bestow Miracles

The woman with mounting debt and no income was instructed by the prophet to borrow as many vessels as she could from neighbors and family members. Then she was instructed to pour whatever oil she had into the vessels and to sell them to pay off her debts and to have money to live off with her family. (See 2 Kings 4:1–7.) God wasn't only interested in fixing her current situation but also in giving her a long-lasting solution. He's interested in giving you a long-lasting solution, too!

The Shunammite woman needed a miracle after her son had died. She chased down the prophet Elisha and asked him to come to her house to pray for her son. When Elisha's servant Gehazi tried to stop the woman from grabbing the prophet, Elisha said that her soul was vexed and to let her come to him. When he heard what had happened to her son, the prophet had compassion. He went to the boy to pray for him and he sought the Lord in prayer to move on behalf of the Shunammite woman until he was able to give the woman's son back to her. (See 2 Kings 4:18–37.) God will do the impossible when He is moved with compassion!

Compassion Moved Jesus to Bestow Miracles

Like Father, like Son—Jesus was moved by compassion! Several times, we read in the Bible that Jesus Himself was moved with compassion for people. One day, a crowd that followed Jesus around as He preached throughout the day grew to five thousand people by dinner time. The Word of God shows us that Jesus looked out at the crowd and felt compassion for them. We read in Matthew,

> *Then Jesus called his disciples unto him, and said, I have compassion on the multitude, because they continue with me now three days, and have nothing to eat: and I will not send them away fasting, lest they faint in the way. And his disciples say unto him, Whence should we have so much*

*bread in the wilderness, as to fill so great a multitude?
And Jesus saith unto them, How many loaves have ye?
And they said, Seven, and a few little fishes. And he commanded the multitude to sit down on the ground. And he
took the seven loaves and the fishes, and gave thanks, and
brake them, and gave to his disciples, and the disciples to
the multitude. And they did all eat, and were filled: and
they took up of the broken meat that was left seven bas-
kets full. And they that did eat were four thousand men,
beside women and children.*   (Matthew 15:32–38)

The disciples were worried about not packing a lunch for
the team, but Jesus didn't worry about what He didn't have to
give the multitude; He focused on what they needed. You can
see that the disciples were consumed with what they didn't
have—food! They even confiscated a kid's lunch, saying,
"Look what we've got!" (See John 6:9.) By that time, Jesus had
already released the miracle, and He was just waiting for it
to manifest in a way of delivery. It could have been chicken
or pizza! It didn't matter; some way, Jesus was going to feed
the multitude that evening. You see, Jesus didn't just logically
ponder what He was going to do with the crowd, consumed
with the fact that they looked so hungry. No, He saw it as a
supernatural moment to release a miracle.

Afterward, the crowd followed Him and sought more
food. But Jesus told them that they sought Him for bread and
not for miracles.

*Jesus answered them and said, Verily, verily, I say unto
you, Ye seek me, not because ye saw the **miracles**, but*

*because ye did eat of the **loaves**, and were filled.*

(John 6:26)

What does this mean? Many people followed Him around only for food, which is a material thing, not a spiritual thing. He knew this because, when He looked at them, He saw their hearts and knew their immediate needs. They needed food not just because they were hungry or because the markets were closed, but because they were poor. These poor people converged on Jesus because they needed bread, not because they had a need for preaching.

Jesus was the original healing Evangelist, pioneering the very thing we do today—feeding the needy! Almost every time I hold an event overseas, my team and I always feed someone—whether at our pastor conferences, crusades, or healing services. Today, I understand the need for it more than I did when I held my first meeting in India.

> THESE POOR PEOPLE CONVERGED ON JESUS BECAUSE THEY NEEDED BREAD, NOT BECAUSE THEY HAD A NEED FOR PREACHING.

On my first trip to Odisha, India, the most dangerous place to preach the gospel in all of India, my team and I prepared a budget to feed three hundred people during the three-day event, which cost about one thousand US dollars. It was all I had raised for that trip; there were no more funds available. I had basically emptied my checking account to hold this small event, and had just enough money in my pocket, three hundred dollars, to pay for things to get home.

When the meeting started, the tent was packed with people. As the service went on, I was informed of an issue: A large group of about two hundred people joined our event at the last minute. They traveled by car six hours from another village called Kandhamal, which had been under religious attacks. It was great that others had joined the meeting, but we had purchased only enough food for three hundred people, not an additional two hundred guests. I noticed how worried and irritated all the staff members were getting about the food supply. In India, when a guest visits, you are obligated to feed them. A snack and tea would suffice; but, again, these were not in our budget.

So I asked my staff members what they wanted to do. They said that they wanted to invite the new guests to stay for the whole three-day conference but that we may only be able to afford a snack and tea for them. That was the last time I heard about the food being an issue. I looked out at the crowd of people laughing, dancing, and enjoying the Lord, and my heart was full of compassion for them. I immediately left the tent meeting along with my head team member and walked straight to the cooks. I told my team member to translate my words exactly as I said them. He agreed.

I told the cooks, "Don't worry about how much food we have or if it will be enough for everyone. Keep cooking, keep preparing, and keep putting food into the containers. Don't look to see what we have to cook—just cook. God will supply!" Then I said to the team who would serve the food, "Don't look into the pots of food wondering if it will be enough. Just serve the food to everyone. God will supply!" Then I looked at all of them, saying, "You keep serving! You keep cooking!"

After, I told my head team member to invite the two hundred visitors to stay for the entire conference. After three days of services, we fed over five hundred people three full meals, two snacks, and tea every day without running out of anything or buying more food. In fact, when I left the compound a few days later, I saw extra food piled up in rows for the cows in the compound to graze upon. Not only did we have enough food for everyone, but we even blessed the cows! Compassion released this miracle of feeding five hundred. Praise God!

Where There Is Compassion, There Are Healings, Miracles, and Salvation

Years ago in India, during the opening night of a conference, I preached about compassion and how it always brings healing and salvation. I shared the story of the men who lowered their paralyzed friend to Jesus through a roof.

And again he entered into Capernaum after some days; and it was noised that he was in the house. And straightway many were gathered together, insomuch that there was no room to receive them, no, not so much as about the door: and he preached the word unto them. And they come unto him, bringing one sick of the palsy, which was borne of four. And when they could not come nigh unto him for the press, they uncovered the roof where he was: and when they had broken it up, they let down the bed wherein the sick of the palsy lay. When Jesus saw their faith, he said unto the sick of the palsy, Son, thy sins be forgiven thee. But there was certain of the scribes sitting there, and reasoning in their hearts, Why doth this man thus speak blasphemies? who can forgive sins but

God only? And immediately when Jesus perceived in his
spirit that they so reasoned within themselves, he said
unto them, Why reason ye these things in your hearts?
Whether is it easier to say to the sick of the palsy, Thy sins
be forgiven thee; or to say, Arise, and take up thy bed, and
walk? But that ye may know that the Son of man hath
power on earth to forgive sins, (he saith to the sick of the
palsy,) I say unto thee, Arise, and take up thy bed, and
go thy way into thine house. And immediately he arose,
took up the bed, and went forth before them all; insomuch
that they were all amazed, and glorified God, saying, We
never saw it on this fashion.　　　　(Mark 2:1–12)

The first time I preached this sermon on compassion in India, the people who heard it responded by inviting others to attend the services the next night. Since then, I have preached this story several times on the first night of healing services, and it continues to bring back larger crowds on the following night.

⌣

I remember a series of videos I watched called *Full Flame* by Reinhard Bonnke. Something I took from them in my spirit was the truth that you get what you preach, so expect it. If you preach healing, you will get healing; if you preach faith, you will get faith; and so on.

The first time I was in Kenya, I preached a sermon about compassion for others. While we prayed for the sick people, a group of five little girls went into a home and grabbed a deaf little girl from the dinner table. They dragged her to me and asked me to pray for her. They had compassion on her because she was deaf. These young girls were about to release a miracle for their friend! Oh, the faith of children!

Four or five of us began to pray for this little girl's healing. When she started making sounds, I told the ministers to stop praying because she had been healed. As soon as we finished praying, the little girl's mother came running up to us and scolded us. She wanted to know why the other girls had taken her daughter away from the dinner table. Through the translator, I told her that the girl was now healed. The woman refused to believe me. Then I then told her to have her daughter say "Momma." The little girl looked at her mother and stuttered, "Momm-ma." The mother fainted. When she got up from the ground, she gave her heart to Jesus.

> PREACHING ON COMPASSION ALWAYS BRINGS HEALINGS AND SALVATIONS.

I got exactly what I preached. Preaching on compassion always brings healings and salvations. Amen!

God Will Make a Way to Reach You

A lame man at the pool of Bethesda was sick for thirty-eight years, and no one helped him. In fact, many just passed him by on their way to the pool. How many people have we passed over, ignoring their needs for miracles? It is because we are too focused on our needs that we forget to help others? Most people sought out Jesus to get healed, but Jesus found this lame man by the pool and had compassion on him. In John, we read,

Now there is at Jerusalem by the sheep market a pool, which is called in the Hebrew tongue Bethesda, having five porches. In these lay a great multitude of impotent folk, of blind, halt, withered, waiting for the moving of the water. For an angel went down at a certain season into the pool, and troubled the water: whosoever then first after the troubling of the water stepped in was made whole of whatsoever disease he had. And a certain man was there, which had an infirmity thirty and eight years. When Jesus saw him lie, and knew that he had been now a long time in that case, he saith unto him, Wilt thou be made whole? The impotent man answered him, Sir, I have no man, when the water is troubled, to put me into the pool: but while I am coming, another steppeth down before me. Jesus saith unto him, Rise, take up thy bed, and walk. And immediately the man was made whole, and took up his bed, and walked: and on the same day was the sabbath. (John 5:2–9)

This man spent many years waiting by the pool for a miracle. We have to ask ourselves these simple questions. Did he even try to get into the pool? Why didn't anyone around help him? Did he know that he would never get into the pool? If so, why did he wait there?

Jesus walked up to this man and directly asked him questions. Now, while there were many sick people around the pool waiting for water pool to be stirred, no one came over to Jesus, and He didn't approach anyone but the lame man. This is one of the very few occasions Jesus searched out someone who needed a healing. He knew that this man had been in this situation for a very long time. (See verse 6.) It didn't matter to Christ if this man had been seeking a healing or if he even knew that Jesus had come over there to heal him. Jesus probably knew that, after thirty-eight years of lying there, the lame man would probably lie there another thirty-eight years before dying. Jesus was moved by compassion for him. Don't you love our Jesus? He is real and has real compassion for others. Compassion for others releases miracles on their behalf.

Compassion for Others Releases Miracles

On my radio show, I interviewed a pastor who had traveled with me on a recent trip to India. I asked Pastor Jorge Vargas what miracle most stood out to him from the trip. He surprised me by telling me of a miracle I didn't even remember. It was when I had jumped out of the jeep and had prayed for a crooked man on the street. I had been traveling through the streets with my ministry team, and I had been half asleep when I'd awaken and, in Hindi, had spoken to my driver to stop the jeep. Then I had jumped out of a very high traffic area and run across the street to a man lying on the ground. In Hindi, I had asked him why he had been lying on the ground. He'd said it was because he was lame and couldn't move. I'd told him to rise up and walk. The man had immediately stood up, picked up his bed, and walked away. His crooked body had been made straight and completely healed! After, I'd gotten back into the jeep and had gone back to sleep.

Let me make two things clear: I didn't remember this miracle, and I don't speak Hindi. God had compassion on this man lying on the street. He knew that no one would take him to a meeting to be healed. He knew that he had suffered with this infirmity for many years. Perhaps He thought that this man would lie there for many more years before dying. But God, through His great compassion, knew I was going to pass by him, and He moved through me during my slumber. In the book of Job, we read,

> *For God speaketh once, yea twice, yet man perceiveth it not. In a dream, in a vision of the night, when deep sleep falleth upon men, in slumberings upon the bed; then he openeth the ears of men, and sealeth their instruction.*
>
> (Job 33:14–16)

During times of slumber, God opens our ears and gives instruction. I can tell you that, many times in my life, God has spoken to me in my slumber. Slumber is that in-between stage of being awake and falling asleep. Once while I was on vacation, God spoke a word audibly to me for three days in a row at 8:43 AM. Those three experiences shaped the way I do things in my ministry today. After that summer vacation, my ministry took off around the world in the areas of broadcasting, missions, and books.

Likewise, during my slumber in the jeep in India, God awakened me and gave me instruction to heal a lame man out of compassion. God can touch you for a miracle in the same way! He's a wonderful, loving, and sensitive God, and He knows your needs. He knows when we are stuck and can't get where we need to go for help. He will set in motion a plan and will use whomever He needs around you to release a miracle. No one is beyond His reach in the world, even the man who lay in a village street in India. God saw him, knew his need, and found a way to deliver it. Amen!

It's awesome that God knows our need and how to get it to us!

CHAPTER 7

COMING TO GOD IGNITES MIRACLES

Faith Is Ignited When People Come to God for Miracles

Special miracles are released when people seek out God for a touch. Faith is put into motion the minute they start believing that God will do something for them. Faith ignites the minute people call on the name of the Lord for His attention. Faith looks different depending on the circumstance. It could manifest in a shout, as in the case of Bartimaeus, who cried out to Jesus for mercy, or even a gentle touch, as in the case of the bleeding woman, who reached out to grab Jesus' garment as He passed in the crowd. Either way, faith is ignited when someone believes, steps out in faith, and gets before the Lord.

One day, I was preparing for a healing service and reading through the miracles of Jesus. I was drawn specifically to the miracles Jesus performed for people who approached Him. As I studied these miracles, I noticed that the people who believed were healed—every one of them! That really stuck in my spirit. After that study, I started realizing the power of faith, and that it ignites when people seek the Healer. Faith begins to elevate even when people start planning to approach Him.

Look at the story of blind Bartimaeus in the Bible. He was with others begging on the street when he heard that Jesus was passing through the city; he must have believed that he could be healed, because he began crying out to Jesus to have mercy on him.

> *And they came to Jericho: and as [Jesus] went out of Jericho with his disciples and a great number of people, blind Bartimaeus, the son of Timaeus, sat by the highway side begging. And when [Bartimaeus] heard that it was Jesus of Nazareth, he began to cry out, and say, Jesus, thou son of David, have mercy on me. And many charged him that he should hold his peace: but he cried the more a great deal, Thou son of David, have mercy on me. And Jesus stood still, and commanded him to be called. And they call the blind man, saying unto him, Be of good comfort, rise; he calleth thee. And he, casting away his garment, rose, and came to Jesus. And Jesus answered and said unto him, What wilt thou that I should do unto thee? The blind man said unto him, Lord, that I might receive my sight. And Jesus said unto him, Go thy way; thy faith hath made thee whole. And immediately he received his sight, and followed Jesus in the way.* (Mark 10:46–52)

Bartimaeus sat on the ground, yelling and crying out to Jesus, recognizing Him as the Messiah. As others tried to shut him up, he cried louder and louder. Jesus asked Bartimaeus what He could do for him, for He recognized the faith that was on the man. Then Jesus told him that his faith had made him whole.

My friends, sometimes, we need to make some noise for Jesus. Cry out to Him! He will hear you! As a minister, I can tell you that I have seen when faith is all over a person; and in that moment, if he asks anything of God, it will be done.

> SOMETIMES, WE NEED TO MAKE SOME NOISE FOR JESUS. CRY OUT TO HIM! HE WILL HEAR YOU!

When I visited an area in India in which I had preached a year earlier, two special miracles happened. When I was shaking hands with and waving good-bye to all the kids at the end of the service, I noticed a young teenage girl who stood behind the other kids and stared at me. At first, I thought she was waiting in line to shake my hand to say good-bye, but when she got up to me and I reached out my right hand to shake hers, she gently took hold of my hand and placed it on her ear. Then she slowly motioned for me to place my other hand on her left ear. After, she put her hands together in a prayer-like fashion. It dawned on me that she was deaf and wanted prayer. At that moment, her friend who stood by her said in English that she is deaf. She continued telling me that the teenage girl had been deaf since she was born and wanted prayer.

So I started to pray for this beautiful young Indian girl. As I prayed, tears started to trickle down from her eyes, and she started repeating every word I said in English. I could see that her faith had been ignited and that she was ready to receive her miracle. She was healed according to her faith, which she had purposed in her heart to put in motion. God is an awesome God!

God Knows Our Deepest Desires

After I prayed for the Indian girl, I was called back to the stage by my India ministry coordinator, Surya, whom we call Shadrach. He kept yelling, "Dr. Gee, Dr. Gee...," which is a term of respect in India. I went onstage and saw him pointing to an older Indian lady. He said that, a year ago, I had prayed for this woman to have a child within the next year because she had been barren and wanted a baby. This older lady had loved Jesus all her life but had never been able to have a baby. I'd told her that she would have a baby boy. The woman was now holding a brand-new baby boy!

God honors faith and the words that we speak. Jesus said that if we believe, we shall have whatever we say. (See, for example, 1 John 5:15.) Bishop Mike Renteria, who was traveling with me, asked the older lady what she had named the child. She said that the child had no name, because God had told her that the man of God who had prayed over her would be back to name the child. The odds of me visiting the same village within a year's time were so slim. In fact, this was the first time I revisited a remote mountain village area in five years of India missions.

Standing in front of the child, I really didn't know what to name him. Then I just said Samuel! The minute I said that,

Bishop Mike took a few steps back and then prophesied over the boy, that he would be a prophet to this region for the Lord and that he would win many to the Lord. God had honored the woman who had come forward for prayer and sought Him for that miracle.

Similarly, as we prepare for the healing part of my services, I encourage people to come forward to receive a miracle from Jesus. I tell them to walk in faith just as the many people in the Bible who went to Jesus and were healed. There is something special about walking to the altar, being in front of God, and crying out to Him that releases faith in the atmosphere.

> THERE IS SOMETHING SPECIAL ABOUT WALKING TO THE ALTAR, BEING IN FRONT OF GOD, AND CRYING OUT TO HIM THAT RELEASES FAITH IN THE ATMOSPHERE.

I held a healing service in a church in Baytown, Texas. I was working through the prayer line when I came to a woman who couldn't stand up but for a few seconds. So I told her to sit down so that I could pray for her. She refused to sit because she believed that if she could stand long enough for me to pray for her, she would be healed. For twenty years, this woman couldn't stand or walk normally; she had to have others pick her up or use a walker. But, even with assistance, it was hard for her to stand for long. She had no strength in her arms and back, either. So I prayed for her really quick, then continued through the prayer line. As I prayed for others, Pastor Benny motioned for me to look at the corner of the room. The woman who hadn't been able to stand was now jumping around, exercising and cheering. Amen! God meets you when you meet Him!

Faith That Catches Jesus' Attention

If you have faith that catches Jesus' attention, it may produce a miracle. As you read the following passage of Scripture, think about this truth. Look at what happened to the woman who sought Jesus to cast out the demon from her daughter. Her faith released blessings from God. We read in the Bible,

> For a certain woman, whose young daughter had an unclean spirit, heard of him, and came and fell at his feet: the woman was a Greek, a Syrophenician by nation; and she besought him that he would cast forth the devil out of her daughter. But Jesus said unto her, Let the children first be filled: for it is not meet to take the children's bread, and to cast it unto the dogs. And she answered and said unto him, Yes, Lord: yet the dogs under the table eat of the children's crumbs. And he said unto her, For this saying go thy way; the devil is gone out of thy daughter. And when she was come to her house, she found the devil gone out, and her daughter laid upon the bed.
>
> (Mark 7:25–30)

The woman in the story refused to be sent away without a blessing. She found Jesus even when He was trying to rest. It wasn't yet time for the Gentiles to receive the gospel; but she still stepped in front of the children of promise to get her blessing.

People have stopped me for prayer in the streets or outside churches in India, Africa, and the US. One time, in the middle of a healing service, an Indian woman pushed through a crowd that had been waiting for prayer and demanded that I immediately pray for her. She was deaf. That particular afternoon was crazy; the people were crowding around me, and my translator was pushed back to the stage. People were complaining and yelling at this lady to go back to the end of the line, but she refused! So I did what she'd asked. She may not have asked for prayer the polite way or the socially correct way, but I prayed for her nonetheless, because of her great faith and boldness. And she was healed immediately! My translator finally caught up to me after pushing through the crowd. I told him that the woman I'd just prayed for was healed. He looked at me puzzled and told me that it was impossible, because that woman was his grandmother and she was deaf. His grandmother hit him with her bag and yelled at him. He laughed because he had been scolded by his grandmother. She was healed—amen!

Two Very Special Miracles

On one of my many trips to a village deep in the mountains of Odisha, India, God worked two very special miracles through me. After ministering to a small church, Bishop Mike and I were resting and drinking a Sprite when a lady with a crooked, mangled arm came up to us. Her forearm was completely twisted and looked horrible. Bishop Mike asked me if I had this one. I cupped my hands like a ball and spread my fingers wide; then I told her to place her arm through my hands. As she passed her hand through my fingers, we saw her hands begin to straighten. We also could hear cracking and popping. By the time she ran her whole arm through my hands, she was completely healed. Bishop Mike said that he could see a fireball in my hands as she passed her arm through my fingers. God had healed her in a creative way. She thanked me, and I connected her with a ministry team to pray for and counsel her. Amen!

As we gathered by the jeep to go back to our hotel, we saw a person calling us from far-off down the road. It was a young girl who was laboring to walk to us. Shadrach suggested we go to her, but I suggested we let her come to us so her faith could make her whole. The people around me thought I was the meanest person because, as she got closer to us, we could see that one of her legs wasn't completely grown. Her foot was near her knee, and she actually used her hands to balance herself as she walked. When she finally made it to us, I asked her what she sought the Lord for. She began to cry, saying that she believed that if she could make it to me before I left, and stand in front of me for prayer, she would be healed. I told her that her faith had made her whole; then I reached down to grab her shorter foot and pulled it to the ground. She kept crying and crying, thanking the Lord for the miracle. Onlookers in the entire area were completely silent and shocked at what had just happened in front of them. I made sure to assign her to a ministry team that would keep up with her. She was a believer who had purposed in her heart to seek the Lord and believe, and she was healed. Amen!

God does the impossible when we believe!

CHAPTER 8

GOD CAN TOUCH ANYONE

One of the most interesting things that I have come across in the healing ministry is that people who are not saved, or who do not fully understand faith, are healed. I have also seen people who know nothing about God receive healings and miracles. These people don't even read the Bible, much less understand it. Some might even say that these people do not deserve or qualify for a touch by God. How could they be healed? They didn't pray or call out to God, so why would He touch them? It might even seem unfair that God touches unbelievers. Surely He sees that His children who truly love and follow Him need healing. Doesn't the Word say that a person needs faith to be healed? Why, then, are unbelievers healed? Something I learned early in my ministry is that God is God, and He can touch whomever He wants, whenever He wants. We read in Romans 9:14–16,

> *What shall we say then? Is there unrighteousness with God? God forbid. For he saith to Moses, I will have mercy*

on whom I will have mercy, and I will have compassion on whom I will have compassion. So then it is not of him that willeth, nor of him that runneth, but of God that sheweth mercy.

AT ANY GIVEN TIME, GOD CAN TOUCH WHOMEVER HE WANTS. HE CAN INTERVENE IN ANYONE'S LIFE AT ANY TIME, WITHOUT INTRODUCTION OR PERMISSION.

In the simplest explanation, God can touch whomever He wants to touch because He is God! God has chosen whom He's chosen throughout the Word of God; He chose Moses, David, Elijah, Ezekiel, Noah, Elisha, Jonah, Abraham, Sampson, Samuel, Nathan, Gideon, Ruth, Deborah, Esther and many other heroes of faith without giving an explanation why, because He is God. So, at any given time, God can touch whomever He wants. He can intervene in anyone's life at any time, without introduction or permission. In the book of Matthew, we read how God even takes care of the birds and the flowers every day without asking them for permission. Why? He takes care of what He creates.

Behold the fowls of the air: for they sow not, neither do they reap, nor gather into barns; yet your heavenly Father feedeth them. Are ye not much better than they? Which of you by taking thought can add one cubit unto his stature? And why take ye thought for raiment? Consider the lilies of the field, how they grow; they toil not, neither do they spin: and yet I say unto you, That even Solomon in all his glory was not arrayed like one of these. Wherefore, if God so clothe the grass of the field, which to day is, and to morrow is cast into the oven, shall he not much more clothe you, O ye of little faith? Therefore take no thought, saying, What shall we eat? or, What shall we drink? or, Wherewithal shall we be clothed? (For after all these things do the Gentiles seek:) for your heavenly Father knoweth that ye have need of all these things.

(Matthew 6:26–32)

Some of the stories I share in this book are of God just stepping into someone's life without any invitation or notice. The crooked and paralyzed man who lay on the street in India needed healing, and God made a way to touch him by awaking me from my sleep and sending me to him. The woman in Kenya was going to the soccer field to kill herself, but God stepped in to her life by putting me in the right place at the right time as I was holding a healing service. Both these people were in rough situations, and only God could see what they needed. He reached out to them and changed their lives forever. We see this happen in the Word of God many times. God just intervenes and changes someone's life. One instance is Peter's encounter with the crippled man at the gate called Beautiful. We read in the book of Acts:

Now Peter and John went up together into the temple at the hour of prayer, being the ninth hour. And a certain man lame from his mother's womb was carried, whom they laid daily at the gate of the temple which is called Beautiful, to ask alms of them that entered into the temple; who seeing Peter and John about to go into

the temple asked an alms. And Peter, fastening his eyes
upon him with John, said, Look on us. And he gave heed
unto them, expecting to receive something of them. Then
Peter said, Silver and gold have I none; but such as I have
give I thee: in the name of Jesus Christ of Nazareth rise
up and walk. And he took him by the right hand, and
lifted him up: and immediately his feet and ankle bones
received strength. And he leaping up stood, and walked,
and entered with them into the temple, walking, and leap-
ing, and praising God.   (Acts 3:1–8)

Mercy Miracles Show He's God

On a break from my radio show, as I got ready for the
second-segment guests, I looked at my cell phone to check my
messages and saw several missed calls from my sister and a
text that said to call her for prayer. After my show, I ran to get
some lunch and called her on the way. She told me that her
boyfriend was very sick and was in the emergency room, and
that he had gotten X-rays taken because his breathing was
limited and he was spitting out blood. The doctors decided
to send him to a specialist to determine what was wrong. I
prayed for him while they were driving to the appointment
with the specialist, and I told him that God would do whatever for him if he believed. After praying for him, I went back
to the station for a TV interview.

A couple of hours later, I called my sister to check on her
boyfriend, and she told me that the doctors couldn't find anything wrong with him. God had healed him, and his symptoms were completely gone. Amen! My sister's boyfriend
didn't know God, but God moved on his behalf.

God Heals Even Those Who Persecute His Children

In Kenya, during the Mwiki Crusade, a certain woman listened to our services from a distance. She had been known in that area to stir up trouble and discord among the churches. During our testimony night, she came onstage to share a testimony. She said that, for many years, her feet had been burning so badly that she couldn't walk without socks. She said that it felt like her feet had been on fire. On one of the nights she'd been listening to our services, God had healed her feet. She testified that she was completely healed and could walk normally. She also said that she would now attend church to be a blessing to the body. Amen! God has mercy on whom He has mercy!

Man Returns from Being Brain-Dead

My cousin texted me on my cell phone to tell me that a family friend had been in an accident and was hospitalized. I asked him to keep me informed and told him that I was praying for him. Around 6 AM, I followed up with a text to check on his condition. My cousin told me that the doctors had said our friend was brain-dead. I reached out in prayer for him, asking God to intervene in his life at this very moment. Later that morning, I got a text that said our friend was awake and eating food. God is good! He hears our prayers and moves on our behalf.

The Bible says in James 5:16, "*The effectual fervent prayer of a righteous man availeth much.*"

Believe that God answers prayer!

CHAPTER 9

INTERCESSION MIRACLES

Throughout my life, people always asked me to pray for their sick friends or family members who were located somewhere else. Even people in my prayer lines ask me to pray for others for a miracle. Sometimes I will get a phone call or an e-mail with requests for prayer. This type of prayer is known as intercessory prayer. God moves strongly through intercessory prayers. We have all been called to be intercessors. We all are called to pray for our families, friends, government, and so on. There is something so special about God moving in response to a person's intercession for someone else. Something happens in the atmosphere when you and I agree in faith for someone else.

> Verily I say unto you, Whatsoever ye shall bind on earth
> shall be bound in heaven: and whatsoever ye shall loose
> on earth shall be loosed in heaven. Again I say unto you,
> That if two of you shall agree on earth as touching any
> thing that they shall ask, it shall be done for them of my

Father which is in heaven. For where two or three are gathered together in my name, there am I in the midst of them.   (Matthew 18:18–20)

When I was a young man in my twenties, I had a reputation of being a man of prayer. People would call me to ask for prayer because they believed that God would answer my request. Most of the time, He would. It was amazing!

One day, a friend called me and asked if I would go with her to pray for a coworker in the hospital. It was my birthday, so I was kind of reluctant about going, but then I thought, *Who am I to decide when God will use me?* I felt that I needed to pray for this man, so I agreed to go. He'd had a severe heart attack, and the doctors were not sure if he would last the night. When we got to the hospital, his family and coworkers were in the hallway quietly mourning together. My friend mentioned to the other that she had brought me here to pray for their friend/family member. I asked the nurse if they had a chapel or any other room that we could use. The group was very large, so the nurse took us to the chapel nearby. I unknowingly took control of the atmosphere by asking everyone in the room to agree with me and believe that their friend or family member would be healed. I told them that God would honor the prayer of the people here who interceded for their friend.

After leading them in a prayer, the family asked me to please visit him in the room. When I went there, he lay in the bed with tubes around him and was laboring to breathe. I laid my hands on him and quietly prayed that God would honor the request of the people praying for him.

The following morning, I got a call from my friend who told me that the man had woken up with no major issues and had been released from the hospital. The doctors were amazed at his recovery. God answers the intercessor's prayers! Intercession has always moved God.

Look at what happened when Abraham prayed for Lot:

> And [Abraham] *said, Oh let not the* LORD *be angry, and I will speak yet but this once: Peradventure ten shall be found there. And he said, I will not destroy* [the city] *for ten's sake. And the* LORD *went his way, as soon as he had left communing with Abraham: and Abraham returned unto his place.* (Genesis 18:32–33)

Abraham interceded for the city before God, and Lot was saved because of his intercessory prayers. The two angels God had sent to visit the land eventually spared Lot by leading him out of the city.

The Centurion's Servant

> And when Jesus was entered into Capernaum, there came unto him a centurion, beseeching him, and saying, Lord, my servant lieth at home sick of the palsy, grievously tormented. And Jesus saith unto him, I will come and heal him. The centurion answered and said, Lord, I am not worthy that thou shouldest come under my roof: but speak the word only, and my servant shall be healed. For I am a man under authority, having soldiers under me: and I say to this man, Go, and he goeth; and to another, Come, and he cometh; and to my servant, Do this, and he doeth it. When Jesus heard it, he marvelled,

and said to them that followed, Verily I say unto you, I have not found so great faith, no, not in Israel. And I say unto you, That many shall come from the east and west, and shall sit down with Abraham, and Isaac, and Jacob, in the kingdom of heaven. But the children of the kingdom shall be cast out into outer darkness: there shall be weeping and gnashing of teeth. And Jesus said unto the centurion, Go thy way; and as thou hast believed, so be it done unto thee. And his servant was healed in the selfsame hour.   (Matthew 8:5–13)

The centurion came to Jesus on the behalf of someone else's need. He understood that Jesus had authority. Even before the centurion went to Jesus to ask Him to heal his servant, he already believed in Him. Scripture says that Jesus marveled at his faith. When you go to God asking and believing for someone else, miracles happen.

A Son Intercedes for His Father

At the radio studio one day, my phone kept ringing, but I couldn't answer it because I was live on-air. When the show was finished, I saw that I had a few text messages from my mother. She said that my dad had gone to the specialist because he had gotten a bad report from his cardio doctor about his heart. Before I called her back, I prayed for my dad. He had always loved us, cared for us, and provided for us since he'd come into our lives when I was five years old, after my natural father had gone to heaven.

I sought the Lord earnestly for him, saying, "Dear Lord, You gave him to us as a blessing to take care of us and to love us. I know that You don't want to take him from us now, so I pray and believe that his heart will be healed today." Immediately after that prayer to the Lord, I called my mom. I told her that Dad would be fine but to let me pray for him over the phone. I told my dad that he was a gift from God to us and that we weren't ready to let that gift go. After praying, I went back to the studio to finish recording my TV show. Later, I got a call from my mother, who said that the specialist couldn't find anything wrong with Dad's heart, and that they didn't know why the cardio doctor had sent him over. God heals when you bring someone to Him in earnest prayer!

A Father Intercedes for His Daughter

I was driving to lunch one day when I got a call from a good friend. He said something to me that has stayed with me even until this day. He told me that I was a healer, and that God had anointed me with a gift to heal. When a person has car trouble, he takes it to a mechanic to get fixed, because that's the mechanic's gifting and talent. Although we *all* can pray for the sick and see them recover, God has anointed and given some people the gift of healing.

> ALTHOUGH WE *ALL* CAN PRAY FOR THE SICK AND SEE THEM RECOVER, GOD HAS ANOINTED AND GIVEN SOME PEOPLE THE GIFT OF HEALING.

Then this man said that his daughter was going to a doctor's appointment today to get some more testing. They had already confirmed that she had cancer but still needed to do more tests. He asked me to pray for her to be completely healed. I was so moved by his faith in understanding and recognition of the gifts of God that I prayed a simple prayer for his daughter and we both agreed that she would be completely healed.

The next day, I got a call from my friend, who was very excited. He said that the doctors didn't find any cancer in her body! God moves through intercessory prayers!

Sisters Intercede for a Brother

Now a certain man was sick, named Lazarus, of Bethany, the town of Mary and her sister Martha. (It was that Mary which anointed the Lord with ointment, and wiped his feet with her hair, whose brother Lazarus was sick.) Therefore his sisters sent unto him, saying, Lord, behold, he whom thou lovest is sick. When Jesus heard that, he said, This sickness is not unto death, but for the glory of God, that the Son of God might be glorified thereby. Now Jesus loved Martha, and her sister, and Lazarus.

(John 11:1–5)

Martha and Mary acted just as any one of us would do for a family member. They sent word to Jesus to come and intercede for their brother so he would be healed. They knew that Lazarus was near death but believed that Jesus could heal him. Then we read,

When Jesus therefore saw her weeping, and the Jews also weeping which came with her, he groaned in the spirit, and was troubled. And said, Where have ye laid him? They said unto him, Lord, come and see. Jesus wept. Then said the Jews, Behold how he loved him! And some of them said, Could not this man, which opened the eyes of the blind, have caused that even this man should not have died? Jesus therefore again groaning in himself cometh to the grave. It was a cave, and a stone lay upon it. Jesus said, Take ye away the stone. Martha, the sister of him that was dead, saith unto him, Lord, by this time he stinketh: for he hath been dead four days. Jesus saith unto her, Said I not unto thee, that, if thou wouldest believe, thou shouldest see the glory of God? Then they took away the stone from the place where the dead was laid. And Jesus lifted up his eyes, and said, Father, I thank thee that thou hast heard me. And I knew that thou hearest me always: but because of the people which stand by I said it, that they may believe that thou hast sent me. And when he thus had spoken, he cried with a loud voice, Lazarus, come forth. And he that was dead came forth, bound hand and foot with graveclothes: and his face was bound about with a napkin. Jesus saith unto them, Loose him, and let him go.   (John 11:33–44)

In this story, you can see just how much Jesus cared for Lazarus and his sisters. He cares for us the same way. He groans and weeps for our intercessory prayer requests even today.

A Mother Intercedes for Her Daughter Through E-mail

The Internet has brought intercessory prayer requests to a whole new level. Years ago, the only way you could submit a prayer requests to a ministry was either by mail or by phone. Nowadays, social networks, contact forms, and e-mails are filled with prayer requests.

Through my Web site, www.davidyanezministries.com, I received a contact form from a mother who wanted me to pray for her daughter who was going through a difficult diagnosis. She asked if we would pray that all her symptoms would be gone and that, at her next appointment with the doctor, she would have a clear report. I personally prayed for her, sent her an e-mail thanking her for contacting me, and told her that I agreed with her in faith for her request.

I personally try to answer as many prayer requests that are submitted to my ministry, whether electronically or by regular mail, as possible. In fact, if you call my prayer line, you will probably end up talking to me. I always make myself available to pray for those who call my ministry.

A month or so went by after I'd prayed for the woman's daughter when I got an e-mail from her. She testified that her daughter's report had come back completely clear and that she no longer had any more symptoms. Praise God that He honors the faith of people who submit online prayer requests in search of someone who will agree with them in intercessory prayer.

Intercessory prayer requests through e-mail, Web site forms, and ministry social media get answered by Jesus!

CHAPTER 10

CREATIVE MIRACLES

In my services in India, I have seen an amazing growth in the number of creative miracles. What are creative miracles? They are miracles that are inspired at the very minute you do something out of the ordinary or supernatural for someone. Creative miracles happen out of necessity. They are inspired by the Holy Spirit but invented, thought up, or orchestrated by the man or woman of God who holds a service. Most creative miracles happen when a need arises that seems difficult or impossible to manage because of time, space, or natural limits. Spirit-inspired instructions for how to meet these needs may not make any sense at all. But your passion and belief drives those around you to follow your lead. The Spirit who guides you will honor your inspired creativity. Miracles happen as you hold on to your faith, believing in the steps you are creating.

Creative Miracles in the Bible

Creative miracles are everywhere throughout the Word of God. There are many examples of God honoring a man of

God's creativity. Look at the following example of Elijah, who challenged the prophets of Baal.

Then said Elijah unto the people, I, even I only, remain a prophet of the LORD; but Baal's prophets are four hundred and fifty men. Let them therefore give us two bullocks; and let them choose one bullock for themselves, and cut it in pieces, and lay it on wood, and put no fire under: and I will dress the other bullock, and lay it on wood, and put no fire under: and call ye on the name of your gods, and I will call on the name of the LORD: and the God that answereth by fire, let him be God. And all the people answered and said, It is well spoken. And Elijah said unto the prophets of Baal, Choose you one bullock for yourselves, and dress it first; for ye are many; and call on the name of your gods, but put no fire under. And they took the bullock which was given them, and they dressed it, and called on the name of Baal from morning even until noon, saying, O Baal, hear us. But there was no voice, nor any that answered. And they leaped upon the altar which was made. And it came to pass at noon, that Elijah mocked them, and said, Cry aloud: for he is a god; either he is talking, or he is pursuing, or he is in a journey, or peradventure he sleepeth, and must be awaked. And they cried aloud, and cut themselves after their manner with knives and lancets, till the blood gushed out upon them. And it came to pass, when midday was past, and they prophesied until the time of the offering of the evening sacrifice, that there was neither voice, nor any to answer, nor any that regarded. And Elijah said unto all the people, Come near unto me. And all the people came near unto him. And

*he repaired the altar of the LORD that was broken down.
And Elijah took twelve stones, according to the number of
the tribes of the sons of Jacob, unto whom the word of the
LORD came, saying, Israel shall be thy name: and with the
stones he built an altar in the name of the LORD: and he
made a trench about the altar, as great as would contain
two measures of seed. And he put the wood in order, and
cut the bullock in pieces, and laid him on the wood, and
said, Fill four barrels with water, and pour it on the burnt
sacrifice, and on the wood. And he said, Do it the second
time. And they did it the second time. And he said, Do
it the third time. And they did it the third time. And the
water ran round about the altar; and he filled the trench
also with water. And it came to pass at the time of the
offering of the evening sacrifice, that Elijah the prophet
came near, and said, LORD God of Abraham, Isaac, and
of Israel, let it be known this day that thou art God in
Israel, and that I am thy servant, and that I have done all
these things at thy word.*   (1 Kings 18:22–36)

After taunting them about their god falling asleep because
their sacrifice had not been consumed with fire, Elijah took the
creative miracle up a notch. He told them to empty basins of
water on top of his woodpile to ensure that the wood was wet.
They also dug a deep trench around it, filling it with water.
Then he stepped back, and the whole sacrifice was consumed
and annihilated with fire, including every drop of water in
the trench! Creativity has been at the heart of miracles from
the beginning. God honors the words we speak and the faith
behind those words.

Elisha's Radical Creativity

Elisha was promised that he would have a double portion of Elijah's anointing.

> And Elijah took his mantle, and wrapped it together, and smote the waters, and they were divided hither and thither, so that they two went over on dry ground. And it came to pass, when they were gone over, that Elijah said unto Elisha, Ask what I shall do for thee, before I be taken away from thee. And Elisha said, I pray thee, let a double portion of thy spirit be upon me. And he said, Thou hast asked a hard thing: nevertheless, if thou see me when I am taken from thee, it shall be so unto thee; but if not, it shall not be so. And it came to pass, as they still went on, and talked, that, behold, there appeared a chariot of fire, and horses of fire, and parted them both asunder; and Elijah went up by a whirlwind into heaven. And Elisha saw it, and he cried, My father, my father, the chariot of Israel, and the horsemen thereof. And he saw him no more: and he took hold of his own clothes, and rent them in two pieces. He took up also the mantle of Elijah that fell from him, and went back, and stood by the bank of Jordan; and he took the mantle of Elijah that fell from him, and smote the waters, and said, Where is the LORD God of Elijah? and when he also had smitten the waters, they parted hither and thither: and Elisha went over.
>
> (2 Kings 2:8–14)

Elisha saw Elijah being taken into heaven, and he didn't waste any time using that double portion he'd been given. He went straight to the Jordon, parted the water, and crossed it the same way he had done with Elijah. Furthermore, this creative man of God cured a spring of water in Jericho with salt (see 2 Kings 2:19–22), sent two bears after forty-two kids who had made fun of his bald head (see 2 Kings 2:23–24), lay over a dead child until he came back to life (see 2 Kings 4:32–35), caused an axe head to float (see 2 Kings 6:4–7), multiplied food to satisfy one hundred men (see 2 Kings 4:42–44), saved a school of the prophets from eating poisonous vegetables (see 2 Kings 4:38–41), and many other miracles. Elisha was so creative that, even when he was dead and buried, his bones raised a dead man to life who had been thrown into his grave! (See 2 Kings 13:21.) Was it faith, inspiration, or creativity? Maybe it was a combination of all three!

Jesus Performed Many Creative Miracles

Jesus' first miracle recorded in the New Testament was very creative.

> *And the third day there was a marriage in Cana of Galilee; and the mother of Jesus was there: and both Jesus was called, and his disciples, to the marriage. And when they wanted wine, the mother of Jesus saith unto him, They have no wine. Jesus saith unto her, Woman, what have I to do with thee? mine hour is not yet come. His mother saith unto the servants, Whatsoever he saith unto you, do it. And there were set there six waterpots of stone, after the manner of the purifying of the Jews, containing two or three firkins apiece. Jesus saith unto them, Fill the waterpots with water. And they filled them up to the brim. And he saith unto them, Draw out now, and bear unto the governor of the feast. And they bare it. When*

*the ruler of the feast had tasted the water that was made
wine, and knew not whence it was: (but the servants which
drew the water knew;) the governor of the feast called the
bridegroom, and saith unto him, Every man at the beginning doth set forth good wine; and when men have well
drunk, then that which is worse: but thou hast kept the
good wine until now. This beginning of miracles did Jesus
in Cana of Galilee, and manifested forth his glory; and
his disciples believed on him.* (John 2:1–11)

Jesus creatively took something as simple as water to make
wine. The servants were instructed by his mother to do whatsoever he asked them to do. I am sure they looked at each other
perplexedly when Jesus said to go pour water into the pots and to
take them to the governor. But the passion and creativity of Jesus
mixed with His faith and boldness inspired them to do whatever
He had instructed. Jesus took what He had and made what He
needed. Jesus shows us that creativity is essential to seeing miracles. He demonstrates His creativeness in miracles throughout
the Gospels. We need to follow in Jesus' steps of creativity!

Paul Creatively Follows in Jesus' Footsteps

Look at one example of how the apostle Paul showed the
creativity of Jesus:

*And God wrought special miracles by the hands of Paul:
so that from his body were brought unto the sick handkerchiefs or aprons, and the diseases departed from them,
and the evil spirits went out of them.* (Acts 19:11–12)

Many came to Paul's meetings expecting great miracles,
and Paul felt inspired to reach others who weren't able to come

to his meetings—maybe even those who had trouble getting there.

I travel to remote areas in India to hold miracle services, and I know that it is hard for people in small villages to travel to where we are holding services. People are so spread out, and transportation is very expensive, so it is always hard for our crowds to visit our services. In fact, I have personally paid for drivers, buses, vans, and bikes to pick people up to bring them to our events.

So I can only imagine that, back in Paul's days, traveling far to hear a miracle worker was just as difficult, if not impossible, for some people. Imagine how difficult it would be for the sick or oppressed to travel long distances.

Inspired by the Holy Spirit, Paul told his team to gather aprons. Then he prayed over all the aprons and instructed that they be ripped into pieces to be sent all over the area. The people who received these ripped pieces of cloth were healed, delivered from demons, and received many other miracles. Paul ignited faith by creating anticipation with the torn pieces of cloth. What released the miracle—was it the cloth or the faith behind the cloth? Paul's faith and actions demonstrated to everyone that the same anointing that is in a service can be in a home. He transported the atmosphere of faith from his meetings to people's very own home. You can even say that he was the original televangelist!

Today, televangelists do the same thing through television programs and the Internet, bringing the atmosphere of faith into homes and releasing miracles. Paul used his imagination and took an everyday item inspired by the Holy Spirit to ignite people's faith all over the place.

Creativity on the Mission Field

I remember preaching in a small home my first time in India. The house was packed with over a hundred people. It was hot and dark, but I just preached and believed that God would move. It's amazing where God will show up when you just believe and faithfully go where He sends you. As I prayed for those in the prayer line, I noticed that several people had asked me to pray for them to receive the Holy Spirit. I told each one of them to go stand on the other side of the room so I could pray for them after I'd finished going through the prayer line.

After praying for everyone, I noticed one of my team members waving at me from the corner. He pointed at everyone who had been waiting for me to pray with them to receive the Holy Spirit, and I counted fifty people who stood shoulder to shoulder praying to God for the baptism of the Holy Spirit. I told them to lift up their hands to heaven and that, when I counted to three, all of them would be baptized in the Holy Spirit. After I counted down to three, a mighty wind rushed through the room. Everyone standing in the corner, including my team members, fell to the ground praying in tongues. No one trained me to ask for the baptism of the Holy Spirit that way; I just felt inspired to pray for them that way. I thought of it, instructed them to do it, and believed that God would honor my step of faith. The people obeyed, trusting me and believing for their miracle.

Jedi Moment on the Road to Airport

Nearing the end of one of my visits to India, I traveled by car to the airport five hours away from where I annually go to preach. We had little time for error since I had already left late and had only six hours before my flight took off. (If you have ever been on a mission trip, you would probably agree with me that when it's time to go home, you don't want to miss your plane.) We were on the road for about four hours, having less than an hour to get to the airport, when I noticed that something was not right.

Our driver usually laughed and joked with us as he drove, but, all of a sudden, he got quiet. I asked him what was wrong. He immediately pointed to the cars pulling over on both sides of the road. Then he briefly explained in broken English that the police were closing the road. I asked him what that meant for us, and he replied that no cars were going anywhere for two hours or more. They just shut down the road with no explanation. He was about to pull over and turn off the car with the other hundred or more vehicles, but I ordered him to slowly drive down the middle of the road. All traffic was pulled over, so we were alone on the road, coasting down the middle for several miles. I told everyone in the car to buckle up their seat belts. As we drove down this long road, we saw many cars, motorcycles, and trucks parked alongside it. People were just standing outside their vehicles talking and waiting and looking at us with crazy expressions on their faces as we passed.

When we finally got to the checkpoint, we saw armed police everywhere yelling instructions and pushing people around. My driver almost stopped the car. He was frightened. I looked at him and told my team member to translate my exact words to him. I told him that if we stopped, we would be stuck, so we had to keep moving if we wanted to get out of here. Then I told him to listen to me only and to follow my instruction exactly.

A policeman waved us down to stop. I told my driver to stop but not to say a word. I didn't roll down my window when he looked into the car. With a wave of my hand, I said in English to the policeman, "This is not the car you are looking for; we can go." The policeman looked at me angrily and was about to hit the window with his rifle, but another policeman walked up behind him, tapped him on the shoulder, and said in Hindi, "This is not the car we are looking for; they can go." Then he waved at us to go.

We drove off slowly, and when we turned a corner, I told my driver to speed fast out of there. My driver was so excited and told me that that had been the most amazing thing he had ever seen. He's been my driver for several years, has been to many of my services, and has seen many miracles. Even though he's Hindu, he believes in Jesus. He was so excited about that one miracle and said that it showed him that God was real and that I was God's man.

That day, we made it to the airport earlier than expected, and I got on my flight to catch my connection home. Creative miracles happen out of necessity. I didn't have time to try and figure out what was going on or what to do. I just acted out of inspiration to create a miracle out of faith.

Throughout this book, I have given other examples of creative miracles, such as feeding five hundred people three meals a day for three days and the healing of the twenty-four blind people in my prayer line. Nobody told me how to do these things; I trusted my spirit in the creative process. Likewise, God wants to show Himself strongly for you. The Bible says in 2 Chronicles 16:9, *"For the eyes of the LORD run to and fro* *throughout the whole earth, to **shew himself strong** in the behalf of them whose heart is perfect toward him.*"

God will show Himself strongly on your behalf!

CHAPTER 11

HIGHWAY AND BYWAY MIRACLES

I am always asked where I go in Kenya and India for my mission work. Sometimes, people expect me to talk about the wonderful places I visit. The truth is that I pass through some of the most beautiful places in Kenya and India to get to the most horrible places on earth. I don't go to glorious vacation sites, beautiful, plush churches, or big stadiums. My mission field is in the slums of Nairobi, Kenya, and in the most hazardous mountains and jungles of India. These places are where miracles and healings are needed the most. I call these places the highways and byways of the mission fields. In these places, the people are truly desperate to believe in something because they have nothing else. They live in remote places and will never get the gospel message unless we go.

That if thou shalt confess with thy mouth the Lord Jesus, and shalt believe in thine heart that God hath raised him from the dead, thou shalt be saved. For with the heart

*man believeth unto righteousness; and with the mouth
confession is made unto salvation. For the scripture saith,
Whosoever believeth on him shall not be ashamed. For
there is no difference between the Jew and the Greek: for
the same Lord over all is rich unto all that call upon him.
For whosoever shall call upon the name of the Lord shall
be saved. How then shall they call on him in whom they
have not believed? and how shall they believe in him of
whom they have not heard? and how shall they hear without a preacher? And how shall they preach, except they be
sent? as it is written, How beautiful are the feet of them
that preach the gospel of peace, and bring glad tidings of
good things!*   (Romans 10:9–15)

One thing I love about the highway and byway ministry is
that the people we minister to are ready to explode in faith to
receive miracles. God sends us to these highways and byways
to reach those who are hurting and in need.

*And another said, I have married a wife, and therefore I
cannot come. So that servant came, and shewed his lord
these things. Then the master of the house being angry
said to his servant, Go out quickly into the streets and
lanes of the city, and bring in hither the poor, and the
maimed, and the halt, and the blind. And the servant
said, Lord, it is done as thou hast commanded, and yet
there is room.*   (Luke 14:20–22)

Not My Will, Lord, but Your Will Be Done

In India, I serve in a state called Odisha. It has been one
of the most hostile areas toward Christians over the years.

Besides the heavy persecution in this area, the travel conditions aren't the best, and there is no air-conditioning in homes, hotels, buildings, and churches. The highway and byway mission fields are the hardest areas in which to minister because comforts are very limited. My team and I travel for hours to remote villages, preach all day, and then travel back to our nearest base of operations overnight. There is no hot water for showers and not much food available late at night. Plus, I don't eat the food in these villages under any circumstance, so I lose twenty to thirty pounds each trip. Most of the time, only grace, patience, and love get me through these visits.

On one trip to Odisha, when my team and I just arrived to India after twenty-one hours of travel to start two weeks of ministry in the villages, we loaded into a jeep to travel five more hours to our base. And, for some reason, my friends invited fourteen Indians to join us in the jeep. I was tired and getting very frustrated with all the noise and heat. I even thought to myself, *I could be home eating a sandwich right now.* I was about to reach my boiling point. (We all have those boiling points. How we react [or not react] is completely up to us). That's when a big rig truck pulled in front of us. On the back of it was a bumper sticker that read "God is awesome!" In the middle of India, a Hindu nation, a bumper sticker had just appeared to encourage me. I looked up to heaven with a smile and silently thanked the Lord. *I must decrease, so You may increase. Not my will, Lord, but Your will be done.*

Villagers Wait Hours for Ministry

I have so many stories of miracles and healings that I have seen in the highways and byways of India and Kenya. Villagers have such a hunger for the things of God. When we hold services in small churches, word spreads, and large numbers of people in the entire area visit us in small churches and form lines for prayer so long that they go outside the church into the streets. People bring the sick, lame, blind, and deaf for prayer.

> *And great multitudes came unto him, having with them those that were lame, blind, dumb, maimed, and many others, and cast them down at Jesus' feet; and he healed them.*   (Matthew 15:30)

Complete villages would wait all night for me to visit them for only a few minutes. I remember one year when we were on our way back from preaching to villages, and one of my leaders told me that we had to make a stop at one more place. We had just finished preaching for five days straight, and I was extremely tired and just wanted to find a hotel. I didn't want to go by the place, but my driver said that he knew the people there and that they had waited all night for me. He also said that it was on the way. I told him that we could stop and to wake me up when we got there. We arrived there after midnight. When they woke me up, I looked out the window of the car and saw a crowd of people waiting in the dark and cold for me. It was a humbling experience. We held a small service, and I had everybody walk by me so that I could lay hands on each person there. Their faith was stirred and released miracles because they had waited. God moved tremendously!

Deaf Ears Opened

Working the highway and byway comes with a great price, but the fruit that comes with that sacrifice is so powerful. The healing and miracles in our ministry weren't always like the ones we have today. Today, the opening of blind eyes and deaf ears is a common occurrence. Demons even leap out from people. But I remember the first time I saw a deaf ear opened in Odisha. In a small village in Chhattisgarh, just three hours outside of Sambalpur, our base of operations, I ministered on one of the hottest days I remember—so hot that I tried to stay in the shade as much as possible. In India, whenever a person arrives to a village to minister, the people lead the visitor to the church in a procession with drums, tambourines, and singing. This is usually a long, slow march to a building or tent. So when the villagers led me to a small building in the heat, it was difficult for me to stay cool in the shade. By the time I got up to preach, I was drenched in sweat. I preached the best I could to a crowd that was packed into a small building with no air-conditioning.

When we started the healing service, I lost sight of my translator because the crowd had surrounded me. So I just started praying my way out of the crowd. One older lady I had prayed for started jumping around. She grabbed me and pointed to her ear that had been healed! The translator came up and asked me if I was okay. I told him that this woman had been healed of deafness. He said that it was impossible, because the woman was his grandmother and she had been deaf all his life. Then the grandmother took her purse and smacked her grandson with it, saying to him, "I am healed! I can hear!" He started laughing and praising God with her. Hallelujah!

Bringing Children Out of Orissa's Deadliest Village

In Kandhamal, a six-hour jeep ride from our base, we held six healing services before driving back home overnight. I was the first non-Indian to preach in this area, which required special permission from the government. In 2008, Christians had been attacked in this area by radical Hindus who had burnt Christian churches, businesses, and homes. Many Christian men, including pastors, other church leaders, and tea makers, had been killed. Thus, this slaughtering of Christians became known as the Tea Maker Massacre.

When I visited this area, I saw the graves of Christian men of the churches in front of the village entrances. In some churches I visited, there were no men at all. These places needed Jesus' touch just as much as the other places I visited. I didn't see such great miracles occur in these villages as we see today, but I did see God move mightily among the people.

During my visit, I noticed a large number of kids living in the streets. I asked my team leader what the story was with them. He said that their parents had been killed during the Tea Maker Massacre, so they lived wherever they could find a place to sleep. He also shared with me that the children weren't allowed to go to school because they believed in Jesus. My heart was immediately filled with love and compassion for these kids. Our first two children's homes started with the kids from these villages. I committed to move one hundred kids to our two facilities to start the new children's homes, but I didn't have the money to move the children right at that moment. It was expensive to get the proper documents to move them, as well as to transport them, cover their medical needs, and provide clothing and housing to one hundred kids. I knew it would take a month or so to get everything ready with the paperwork. By then, I would be back in the States, so I had some time to refresh myself and to get the money by faith.

We all need to understand that faith takes time. Sometimes, God does answer immediately, but faith that lasts and continues to produce in a person's life takes time to develop. It was about a month or so after I got back to the States that I received a call from my team in India who gave me the status and the tally of the possible candidates to be moved to the children's homes. I knew faith was about to produce something. God wouldn't have sent me there and put this in my spirit just to abandon these kids now.

I was working on some unrelated ministry things just a few days after talking with my team in India when I got another phone call. This time, it from a longtime friend who had seen a few of my e-mail reports about India. He had regularly followed my ministry and supported my last mission trip, too. He asked what I was doing for the orphans and when was I planning to move them. I told him the projected schedule for the move of the kids, and he asked me to give him an idea of how much I was short on the costs of moving the children and supporting them for the first month. I have learned that, sometimes, it's best not to put a number on a blessing, so I just told him to pray and that anything would be a blessing. A few days later, I received a check from my friend that paid for the entire cost of moving the children and supporting them for a full month. Miracles are released when we look at God and not the deadline.

Twenty-Four Blind People Healed in One Service

Over the years of visiting India, I have noticed that the power of God is more abundant on each trip. Furthermore, I have felt my faith being strengthened and my expectation growing for the people at my services. One service in particular proved it. When we reached the healing part of this service, I asked that everyone who was blind to come to the front for a special prayer. Twenty-five blind people came forward. I asked that they all be placed in a line side by side and told them to close their eyes tight. Then I instructed my team not to touch them but to just walk by them as they prayed for them. After, I counted to three, and told the blind people to open their eyes. Twenty-four of them opened their eyes and were completely healed. Amen! The one who had not been healed believed that her blindness was a gift from God to minister to people about Him. You get what you believe. I instructed my team to stop praying for her, because she needed faith to be healed. Readers, God wants you healed!

Three Hundred Women Baptized in the Holy Spirit in One Service

On that particular trip, the power of God got stronger as we moved to the next village in the mountains. During the praise and worship part of the service, all the women in attendance began to utter a beautiful sound of the Holy Spirit. As three hundred women were filled with the Spirit, they screamed and cried out in the Holy Spirit. In India, the men sit on one side of the church, the women sit on the other side of the church, and the kids in the front. So, imagine all the women, which was about a third of the church, on one side of the room being baptized and filled with the Holy Spirit, as all the men just watched. The pastor didn't understand what was going on; he started yelling at them because he thought they were being disruptive. In almost all the places I have visited in India, the people have never seen the Holy Spirit move in a service. Sometimes, it takes time for them to get comfortable with a healing service; but the way I explain it to them is that, if God wants to touch someone, He will do so because He is God.

Counterfeit Healers in Nairobi, Kenya

> IF GOD WANTS TO TOUCH SOMEONE, HE WILL DO SO BECAUSE HE IS GOD.

In Nairobi, there are so many counterfeit ministries that pretend to operate in the power of God. They set up just to profit from praying for the sick. You will see them in shops along the streets, on radio and television talk shows, and even advertised on billboards with the prices of each miracle. I remember seeing a TV ministry charge five thousand Kenyan shillings (KSh) to heal people with foot injuries, 35,000 KSh to heal people in wheelchairs, and 100,000 KSh to heal people of cancer. This really grieved my spirit to see the gospel being prostituted for money. I now understand how Jesus felt when He walked in on the money changers cheating people in the temple of God.

> *And the multitude said, This is Jesus the prophet of Nazareth of Galilee. And Jesus went into the temple of God, and cast out all them that sold and bought in the temple, and overthrew the tables of the moneychangers, and the seats of them that sold doves, and said unto them, It is written, My house shall be called the house of prayer; but ye have made it a den of thieves.*
>
> (Matthew 21:11–13)

In John, a similar incident is recorded.

And the Jews' passover was at hand, and Jesus went up to Jerusalem. And found in the temple those that sold oxen and sheep and doves, and the changers of money sitting: and when he had made a scourge of small cords, he drove them all out of the temple, and the sheep, and the oxen; and poured out the changers' money, and overthrew the tables; and said unto them that sold doves, Take these things hence; make not my Father's house an house of merchandise. And his disciples remembered that it was written, The zeal of thine house hath eaten me up.

(John 2:13–17)

Holy Zeal and the Demonstration of God's Power

In fact, that same zeal Jesus demonstrated in those temples came over me during the first night of one of my crusades in the slums of Mwiki. Usually, during the ministry part of my services, I send my team of pastors out to lay hands on the crowd. But one particular night, the Lord stopped me from sending them out. Instead, I told them to hold back for a minute while I prayed. Looking at the crowds of people, I prayed that God would show me what He wanted me to do. Then God whispered to me to go pray for the people myself. While I walked down the stairs of the stage, God whispered to me again. He said that there were many in the crowd who had been hurt by those counterfeit ministers. He also said that many of those fake healers were in the crowd watching what we were doing to see if we were real. That holy zeal consumed me immediately!

*For the **zeal** of thine house hath **eaten** me up; and the reproaches of them that reproached thee are fallen upon me.*   (Psalm 69:9)

Handing the microphone to my translator, I then proceeded to the prayer line. Over one hundred people, many who were in dire need of a touch from God, lined up for prayer. Quickly I went through the line, laying hands on each person. The ministry team of pastors and leaders stood behind them as I prayed, catching them as they all fell under God's power.

When I finished, I professed to the crowd that the true and living God was here to heal and deliver and that no man could do what God does! Each person in the line I prayed for was completely healed. God is awesome! God wanted to show these people who had suffered from counterfeits that He was God. He also wanted to show them that no man could do what He can do. There is no cost to God's healing! No price to His miracles!

After this seven-day crusade, I was told that no ministry has ever had such a successful event in this particular slum. This is why I go to the slums of Nairobi and the remote villages of India. God wants to touch these people so strongly with His love, but He needs someone to go.

Someone has to go to remote places to show the people that miracles still happen!

CHAPTER 12

FAITH OVERCOMES FEAR

Recently I started noticing something different happening in all my healing services in the US. In one church in Humble, Texas, there were over two thousand people waiting in a prayer line. Some people waited for a couple of hours for me to pray over them. My heart went out to them for waiting so long for their miracles. In India and Africa, my healing services are usually done really quickly, but I couldn't find a way to speed up this service for the people. Normally, I would go right through the line and pray quickly for all of them; but, lately, God has been having me just pray directly over each person individually.

So, as I went through the prayer line in Humble, I kept getting the same prayer requests from people. They kept requesting that I pray for them because they had such a fear overtaking them for their families and the presence of discord in their families. I didn't think much of it at first; but after I was about midway through the massive line, I realized that something was happening here. A spirit of fear was operating against these people. It was attacking them in their thoughts and dreams as they slept. The Bible says not to panic when fear comes to visit you and your family.

> *When thou liest down, thou shalt not be afraid: yea, thou shalt lie down, and thy sleep shall be sweet. Be not afraid of sudden fear, neither of the desolation of the wicked, when it cometh. For the LORD shall be thy confidence, and shall keep thy foot from being taken.*   (Proverbs 3:24–26)

What is sudden fear? Its panic! Panic will creep into your mind when you think, see, or hear something fearful. Fear will rest on a person, causing him to worry or be afraid. Typically, he will begin acting out in panic, impatience, despair, and unrest. Fear causes people to change what they believe, and it's the opposite of faith. It produces the exact opposite results.

YOUR BELIEF PRODUCES VICTORY OR DEFEAT, PROVISION OR LACK, SICKNESS OR HEALTH, AND LIFE OR DEATH. GOD KNOWS THIS.

What you believe, you will receive! Belief is the basis to our faith. Jesus said many times in the Bible that, as you believe, it will done unto you. (See, for example, Matthew 9:29.) Your belief produces victory or defeat, provision or lack, sickness or health, and life or death. God knows this. In fact, He has given us everything we need to beat fear, because He never intended fear to be a part of our thinking process. In the Bible, we read that God has not given us a spirit of fear.

> *For God hath not given us the **spirit of fear**; but of **power**, and of **love**, and of a **sound mind**.*   (2 Timothy 1:7)

God does not give a spirit of fear. We need to walk with the authority of the power of God, which is given to us through the Holy Spirit. God's love should be strong within our hearts, and our minds should always be resting on His Word. Also, His love for us is so strong that He has already empowered each of us with a portion of faith.

> *For I say, through the grace given unto me, to every man that is among you, not to think of himself more highly than he ought to think; but to think soberly, according as God hath dealt to every man the measure of faith. For as we have many members in one body, and all members have not the same office: so we, being many, are one body in Christ, and every one members one of another. Having then gifts differing according to the grace that is given to us, whether prophecy, let us prophesy according to the proportion of faith; or ministry, let us wait on our ministering: or he that teacheth, on teaching; or he that exhorteth, on exhortation: he that giveth, let him do it with simplicity; he that ruleth, with diligence; he that sheweth mercy, with cheerfulness.*   (Romans 12:3–8)

Paul told the people that each of them had a measure of faith, and to operate in the portion that they had been given. This section of Scripture reminds us that each of us has different gifts and measures of faith. Faith is a constant belief process. A person's faith, at times, may be very strong, enabling him to take on the biggest challenges; then, all of sudden, faith seems leave, leaving a person unable to handle the smallest obstacles. We see this in the story of Elijah who faced Ahab with boldness and confidence, then ran from Jezebel and wished to die.

> *And Elijah said unto Ahab, Get thee up, eat and drink; for there is a sound of abundance of rain. So Ahab went up to eat and to drink. And Elijah went up to the top of Carmel; and he cast himself down upon the earth, and put his face between his knees, and said to his servant, Go up now, look toward the sea. And he went up, and looked, and said, There is nothing. And he said, Go again seven times. And it came to pass at the seventh time, that he said, Behold, there ariseth a little cloud out of the sea, like a man's hand. And he said, Go up, say unto Ahab, Prepare thy chariot, and get thee down that the rain stop thee not. And it came to pass in the mean while, that the heaven was black with clouds and wind, and there was a great rain. And Ahab rode, and went to Jezreel. And the hand of the LORD was on Elijah; and he girded up his loins, and ran before Ahab to the entrance of Jezreel.*
>
> (1 Kings 18:41–46)

> *And Ahab told Jezebel all that Elijah had done, and withal how he had slain all the prophets with the sword. Then Jezebel sent a messenger unto Elijah, saying, So let the gods do to me, and more also, if I make not thy life as the life of one of them by to morrow about this time. And when he saw that, he arose, and went for his life, and came to Beersheba, which belongeth to Judah, and left his servant there. But he himself went a day's journey into the wilderness, and came and sat down under a juniper*

tree: and he requested for himself that he might die; and said, It is enough; now, O LORD, take away my life; for I am not better than my fathers. And as he lay and slept under a juniper tree, behold, then an angel touched him, and said unto him, Arise and eat. And he looked, and, behold, there was a cake baken on the coals, and a cruse of water at his head. And he did eat and drink, and laid him down again. And the angel of the LORD came again the second time, and touched him, and said, Arise and eat; because the journey is too great for thee. And he arose, and did eat and drink, and went in the strength of that meat forty days and forty nights unto Horeb the mount of God. And he came thither unto a cave, and lodged there; and, behold, the word of the LORD came to him, and he said unto him, What doest thou here, Elijah?

(1 Kings 19:1–9)

One day, Elijah was full of faith and, the next day, he was out of faith. Have you ever felt like this? He demonstrated how strong fear can affect a person's life. Fear can take you in a completely opposite direction than faith if you choose to believe in it. Elijah even went into a depression, sleeping excessively and not eating. Fear can cripple a person's faith! It can make you not want to do anything, visit anyone, or eat anything. Elijah still had faith, but it was being overtaken by fear, which meant that his faith was being depleted or low. None of us can lose faith completely, because, by grace, our faith is always with us.

*For by **grace** are ye saved through **faith**; and that not of yourselves: it is the gift of God.*   (Ephesians 2:8)

Elijah eventually had to get a grasp of his situation, refocus his mind on God, and choose to believe again.

Measures of Faith

That's something we all have to do at some time in our walk with God. Faith has different levels of ups and downs, valleys and peaks. We see them throughout the Word of God, especially in the lives of the disciples in the New Testament.

No Faith

Jesus' disciples had seen several miracles while walking with Jesus. But the winds and the storms greatly scared them, completely depleting their faith.

And he arose, and rebuked the wind, and said unto the sea, Peace, be still. And the wind ceased, and there was a great calm. And he said unto them, Why are ye so fearful? how is it that ye have no faith? And they feared exceedingly, and said one to another, What manner of man is this, that even the wind and the sea obey him?

(Mark 4:39–41)

Little Faith

Peter had faith when he walked out on the water, but it began to fade, and he started to sink. Often, when Jesus mentions "*little faith*," He means not enough faith.

But when [Peter] saw the wind boisterous, he was afraid; and beginning to sink, he cried, saying, Lord, save me. And immediately Jesus stretched forth his hand, and caught him, and said unto him, O thou of little faith, wherefore didst thou doubt? And when they were come into the ship, the wind ceased.   (Matthew 14:30–32)

Great Faith

The centurion in Luke chapter 7 and the woman from Canaan in Matthew chapter 15 were the only two people in the Bible whom Jesus said had great faith. He marveled at their understanding, because they understood how faith worked and believed.

[The centurion said,] *For I also am a man set under authority, having under me soldiers, and I say unto one, Go, and he goeth; and to another, Come, and he cometh; and to my servant, Do this, and he doeth it. When Jesus heard these things, he marvelled at him, and turned him about, and said unto the people that followed him, I say unto you, I have not found so great faith, no, not in Israel. And they that were sent, returning to the house, found the servant whole that had been sick.*   (Luke 7:8–10)

And [the woman from Canann] *said, Truth, Lord: yet the dogs eat of the crumbs which fall from their masters' table. Then Jesus answered and said unto her, O woman, great is thy faith: be it unto thee even as thou wilt. And her daughter was made whole from that very hour.*
(Matthew 15:27–28)

Fullness of Faith

Stephen and Barnabas were the only two mentioned in the Bible for their fullness of faith. The Word says that they did great things.

And Stephen, full of faith and power, did great wonders and miracles among the people.   (Acts 6:8)

Then tidings of these things came unto the ears of the church which was in Jerusalem: and they sent forth Barnabas, that he should go as far as Antioch. Who, when he came, and had seen the grace of God, was glad, and exhorted them all, that with purpose of heart they would cleave unto the Lord. For he was a good man, and full of the Holy Ghost and of faith: and much people was added unto the Lord.   (Acts 11:22–24)

> AT ANY TIME IN OUR WALK WITH GOD, WE CAN HAVE NO FAITH, LITTLE FAITH, GREAT FAITH, OR FULLNESS OF FAITH. IT'S ACCORDING TO WHAT WE CHOOSE TO BELIEVE.

So, at any time in our walk with God, we can have no faith, little faith, great faith, or fullness of faith. It's according to what we choose to believe. I have had the privilege of working in the healing ministry for many years. It's been the best job in the world to encourage people's faith and see miracles released around the world.

When You Remove Fear, Great Things Happen!

Here are some examples of faith-released miracles from some of my meetings in the US:

+ An eighty-four-year-old woman's legs were healed. When her doctor asked her why she wasn't using her cane, she told him that she didn't need it because she had faith!

+ A woman who suffered from severe back problems for several years woke up one day completely healed!

+ A woman who could never stand on her own asked me to pray for her and decided that, by faith, she would let go of her walker. She believed that her healing would come in that minute. A few minutes later, she was doing jumping jacks and cheering in the corner!

+ A woman whose face had been paralyzed was healed during my preaching!

+ A woman with rib pain was healed!

+ A woman with fibromyalgia was healed after I'd laid hands on her for prayer. She had fallen to the ground, and when she'd gotten up, she was completely healed.

+ A woman with knee problems fell to ground after prayer, and when she got up, her knee was completely healed!

+ A man was healed of hearing loss!

+ A man's hands were healed of arthritis!

+ A man's injured back was completely healed!

+ A man's injured knee, back, and foot were completely healed after five years of suffering!

+ A woman with only 20 percent of her vision left and was healed completely!

+ A woman with scoliosis in her back was completely healed!

+ A young man had molar issues until I laid hands on his jaw and it began to start popping. He was completely healed!

+ An older woman had heart issues; as we prayed, her heart leaped five times. Her report from her doctor confirmed that she was completely healed.

+ A 94-year-old man who was to have back surgery the next day felt God touch him after we prayed for him. He cancelled the surgery and two days later was working in his garden, completely healed.

+ A woman who was deaf in her right ear was instantly healed when we laid hands on her!

On several occurrences, people have waited in my healing lines just to give me a hug and to tell me that they were healed. People have testified of amazing miracles of healed backs and knees, the opening of blind eyes, and much more during my preaching services. Miracles happen when faith is released in the atmosphere.

Faith will always overpower fear if we don't allow fear to overpower us!

CONCLUSION

MAN'S GREATEST FEAR DEFEATED

We all want to live healthy and financially blessed lives. When we are challenged by sickness or loss, we ask for prayer that God will bless us. Anytime our health or finances suffer, we tend to doubt or fear that our prayers will go unanswered. Fear comes to visit! Fear taunts us, telling us that the healing and miracle we need won't come on time. Fear can be tormenting and merciless. Why do we fear? Could it be that, if we don't get healed, death will follow? The grave is next?

Our greatest fears are death and the grave. I host a yearly TV special on my network called *Survivors by Faith*, on which we share the stories of people who have believed for their miracles for many years. Many of these guests have gone through life with their sickness or disease and have prayed, believed, and trusted God for their healing. We talk about their faith in God during those difficult times to encourage viewers to believe. The last segment on each show is always about someone who has passed away with prayers unanswered. You might think this is a cruel, insensitive thing for us to focus on, but you would be surprised by what people share about their loved ones. Almost all the time, these people share that their loved ones believed that their healing would come even until the last day of their lives. When you believe even when you die, you win! There is no shame in dying while believing! Our last fears on this earth are death and the grave, but Jesus has defeated them both!

> *So when this corruptible shall have put on incorruption, and this mortal shall have put on immortality, then shall be brought to pass the saying that is written, Death is swallowed up in victory. O death, where is thy sting? O grave, where is thy victory? The sting of death is sin; and the strength of sin is the law.*   (1 Corinthians 15:54–56)

Jesus gave us a victory, promising us that no sickness, disease, financial loss, or devastation could ever keep us from. He showed us that He has power over death and the grave. Jesus Himself holds the keys of hell and death.

> *I am he that liveth, and was dead; and, behold, I am alive for evermore, Amen; and have the **keys of hell and of death**.*   (Revelation 1:18)

Jesus showed us that there is nothing to fear. Fear cannot yell loud enough to take away what Jesus has done for us. He holds the key of hell and death. Hell and death have no power over us because He has personally freed us from them. Jesus demonstrated this authority even before His death and resurrection when He raised Lazarus from the grave.

And when he thus had spoken, he cried with a loud voice, Lazarus, come forth. And he that was dead came forth, bound hand and foot with graveclothes: and his face was bound about with a napkin. Jesus saith unto them, Loose him, and let him go.   (John 11:43–44)

God's love makes it possible for us to never fear again. He took all the power of fear away by giving us His Son.

What shall we then say to these things? If God be for us, who can be against us? He that spared not his own Son, but delivered him up for us all, how shall he not with him also freely give us all things? Who shall lay any thing to the charge of God's elect? It is God that justifieth. Who is he that condemneth? It is Christ that died, yea rather, that is risen again, who is even at the right hand of God, who also maketh intercession for us. Who shall separate us from the love of Christ? shall tribulation, or distress, or persecution, or famine, or nakedness, or peril, or sword? As it is written, For thy sake we are killed all the day long; we are accounted as sheep for the slaughter. Nay, in all these things we are more than conquerors through him that loved us. For I am persuaded, that neither death, nor life, nor angels, nor principalities, nor powers, nor things present, nor things to come, nor height, nor depth, nor any other creature, shall be able to separate us from the love of God, which is in Christ Jesus our Lord.

(Romans 8:31–39)

Everyone that has confessed Jesus as his Lord and Savior has taken part in the greatest miracle ever—salvation!

For God so loved the world, that he gave his only begotten Son, that whosoever believeth in him should not perish, but have everlasting life.   (John 3:16)

If you would like to confess Jesus as Lord of your life today, please do so by reciting this short prayer:

Heavenly Father, I am a sinner. Please forgive me for all my sin. I accept Jesus Christ as my Lord and Savior over my life today. Amen.

Watch, stand fast in the faith, be brave, be strong.
                    (1 Corinthians 16:13 NKJV)

APPENDIX

QUICK REFERENCE GUIDE TO HEALING AND MIRACLES

I put together this reference guide to share some of the things I have learned while operating in the healing and miracle ministry. This guide will give you an insight into the mindset and beliefs you must have to see God's Word ignite in your life. Each of these twenty-one items are always thriving in my spirit every day and every hour. These principles are like a battery, constantly supercharging my faith at all times. I believe these are going to supercharge your faith and ignite the miracles in your life and in the lives of others.

1. Confidence

We must have confidence that God will perform miracles for us, personally.

If He won't do it for you, He won't do it for anybody else, either.

Then Peter opened his mouth, and said, Of a truth I per-
ceive that God is no respecter of persons.   (Acts 10:34)

Believe that no matter your situation, He can do it.

2. Jesus' Name Is Powerful

The name of Jesus is the final authority in all things,
period.

In Acts, Peter spoke the name of Jesus at a gate and a man
lame from birth got up and walked. (See Acts 3:1–11.)

Know the power in the name.

That at the name of Jesus every knee should bow, of things
in heaven, and things in earth, and things under the earth;
and that every tongue should confess that Jesus Christ is
Lord, to the glory of God the Father.
                                        (Philippians 2:10–11)

Demons tremble at the sight of Him.

3. Grace Is Unexplainable

Jesus' grace can't be explained, nor can we understand it.
It is both undeserved and unmerited.   It's equally and freely
given to all. All we have to do is receive it.

Don't look back into your past and let it loom over you.

The woman at the well allowed her past to loom over her.
When she met Jesus, she first admitted her past shame: *"I*
have no husband" (John 4:17). In the presence of Jesus, she
immediately thought of her sin instead of His grace. Yet
Jesus surprised her by looking beyond her past, even confess-
ing, *"Thou hast well said, I have no husband: for thou hast had*

five husbands" (verses 17–18). But this didn't keep Him from revealing Himself to her. In other words, it doesn't matter what she had done. Jesus saw it all and forgave it all.

How many of us allow our past lives to taint the happiness and joy that is abundant in our forgiven lives? No matter how wonderful life is, the thoughts of our pasts come back to haunt us.

Know that you are forgiven. God cannot move when your faith is drowning in unworthiness.

> *Even the righteousness of God which is by faith of Jesus Christ unto all and upon all them that believe: for there is no difference: for all have sinned, and come short of the glory of God; being justified freely by his grace through the redemption that is in Christ Jesus: whom God hath set forth to be a propitiation through faith in his blood, to declare his righteousness for the remission of sins that are past, through the forbearance of God; to declare, I say, at this time his righteousness: that he might be just, and the justifier of him which believeth in Jesus. Where is boasting then? It is excluded. By what law? of works? Nay: but by the law of faith.*   (Romans 3:22–27)

4. Commune with God

Spend time with Him.

> *If ye abide in me, and my words abide in you, ye shall ask what ye will, and it shall be done unto you.*   (John 15:7)

When you spend time with God, you will learn to think like Him. Your speech, thoughts, and actions will become different. You will have greater confidence as you dwell with Him. This confidence will allow your faith to believe all the more in His promises.

5. The Word Must Be in You
There is no faith without the Word of God.

So then faith cometh by hearing, and hearing by the word of God. (Romans 10:17)

But without faith it is impossible to please him: for he that cometh to God must believe that he is, and that he is a rewarder of them that diligently seek him. (Hebrews 11:6)

And Jesus said unto them, I am the bread of life: he that cometh to me shall never hunger; and he that believeth on me shall never thirst. (John 6:35)

6. Let the Man of God Believe with You
Something special happens when an anointed man or woman of God believes with you. They have been with God and have empowered themselves with faith.

Many times in ministry events in Kenya I have felt the need to bring the gospel in a strong manner, because of the fake healing ministers that have charged money from the Kenyan people for miracles. When ministering there, I could sense the people's lack of faith. There was a great need for a man of God to boldly come to them in His name and power.

7. The Prayer of Faith

You must look at Jesus when praying the *"prayer of faith,"* not at the sickness, the circumstances, or the person.

> *And the prayer of faith shall save the sick, and the Lord shall raise him up; and if he have committed sins, they shall be forgiven him.*   (James 5:15)

Smith Wigglesworth once said, "You can never pray the *'prayer of faith'* (James 5:15) if you look at the person who is needing it; there is only one place to look, and that is to Jesus."

8. Remember That We Are Invaded

After we are saved, we are washed clean. In fact the best time for healings and miracles to occur is after salvation. The Word of God says that we are clean and without sin. (See 1 John 1:9.) Believers at the time of rebirth are pure. It's a prime time to claim healings and miracles.

Unfortunately, sin, fear, unforgiveness, and lies are ready to invade our spiritual bodies, making us susceptible to sickness, disease, and depression.

Hear what Job had to say about the invasion of fear: *"For the thing which I greatly feared is come upon me, and that which I was afraid of is come unto me"* (Job 3:25).

Jesus gave us a glimpse of what happens when a clean and empty space is invaded by spirits:

> *When the unclean spirit is gone out of a man, he walketh through dry places, seeking rest, and findeth none. Then he saith, I will return into my house from whence I came out; and when he is come, he findeth it empty, swept, and*

garnished. Then goeth he, and taketh with himself seven other spirits more wicked than himself, and they enter in and dwell there: and the last state of that man is worse than the first. Even so shall it be also unto this wicked generation. (Matthew 12:43–45)

When we hold on to unforgiveness, we open ourselves to being invaded. It is up to us to fill ourselves with His presence.

9. Faith in Salvation Is the Same as Faith in Healing

If you have the faith to be saved, not seeing anything but only saying a prayer, then you should know that healing works in exactly the same way. Receiving healing is just as easy as receiving salvation. Just believe!

10. We Must Have Faith in the Word

For unto us was the gospel preached, as well as unto them: but the word preached did not profit them, not being mixed with faith in them that heard it. (Hebrews 4:2)

+ Faith in Jesus
+ Faith in the blood
+ Faith in cleansing power
+ Faith in the healing of the body

11. Faith Has Nothing to Do with Feeling

It's about God's Word, not what you feel.

T. L. Osborn used to say, "Faith has nothing to do with feeling. Feeling has nothing to do with faith." After someone prays for you, it doesn't matter how you feel; it matters how you believe.

The carnal mind listens to what the feelings have to say; the spiritual mind believes the Word of God.

12. Healing Is the Will of God

Your sickness is not from God.

> *If thou wilt diligently hearken to the voice of the* LORD *thy God, and wilt do that which is right in his sight, and wilt give ear to his commandments, and keep all his statutes, I will put none of these diseases upon thee, which I have brought upon the Egyptians: for I am the* LORD *that healeth thee.*   (Exodus 15:26)

Jesus went about doing His Father's will. Jesus only did what God wanted Him to do. Thus, healing is the will of the Father.

13. Be Creative

Paul used handkerchiefs and aprons. Jesus used water. Both used whatever was available to create the miracle that faith was releasing.

> *And God wrought special miracles by the hands of Paul: so that from his body were brought unto the sick handkerchiefs or aprons, and the diseases departed from them, and the evil spirits went out of them.*   (Acts 19:11–12)

> *Jesus saith unto them, Fill the waterpots with water. And they filled them up to the brim.*   (John 2:7)

Let the Spirit guide you when you need to be creative for a situation. During a service in India, I actually climbed out of a church window during prayer in order to open the front doors to pray for the sick as they exited. God honored that move of faith by healing the entire village.

14. Meet People Where They Are in Faith

Faith varies from person to person.

Kenneth Copeland once shared that he had to meet his wife Gloria at her level of faith for her healing from cancer. At that time Kenneth's faith was at a higher level than hers. But on day he asked her what she believed God could do for her healing. She told him where her faith was and he simply agreed with her at that level and prayed. After a short time, she was healed completely of cancer.

You have to meet people where they believe to make faith ignite. My niece, Isabel, suffered with a crooked back and crooked legs, due to a sickness she was born with. On her fourteenth birthday the doctors said she would be passing the age limit at which they would be able to surgically repair her crooked bones. To all of our surprise, she opted for the long and excruciatingly painful surgery. The night before her operation, she asked to come over to my house for prayer. I shared many of the testimonies in this book to help her understand and boost her faith level.

After telling her the testimonies, I asked her, "So what do you believe God can do for you?"

She said, "I believe that God can guide the surgeons to do the surgery quickly and successfully. I don't want to feel any pain, either."

So I prayed with her, agreeing to a quick, successful, and painless surgery. The next day, what was supposed to have been an eight-hour surgery was over in only three hours. When my niece woke up she said she didn't feel any pain during or after surgery. In fact she hasn't been in any pain at all relating to the surgery. Amen!

Watch for the places where you can meet the level of other people's faith in order to ignite a miracle.

15. Sometimes You Will Have to Do Something You Don't Want to Do

Obey God, no matter what.

In Kenya, I was ministering in a small village church. When I started ministering in the prayer lines, I asked a lady what she needed prayer for. She removed a scarf on her neck, revealing a large goiter the size of a grapefruit. I looked at it and my first thought was that I didn't want to touch it. But the Lord told me to touch it. So, with my pinky finger, I softly touched the goiter. As soon as I touched it, the goiter started to shrink. I put my whole hand on it as it continued to shrink until my hand was resting on the woman's fully healed neck. Amen!

Not everything we do is something we want to do, but when you're obedient it opens the door for miracles.

16. Delayed Miracles

Then said he unto me, Fear not, Daniel: for from the first day that thou didst set thine heart to understand, and to chasten thyself before thy God, thy words were heard, and I am come for thy words. But the prince of the kingdom of Persia withstood me one and twenty days: but, lo,

*Michael, one of the chief princes, came to help me; and I
remained there with the kings of Persia.*

(Daniel 10:12–13)

Daniel's prayer was answered the same day.

The devil can't stop it.

The angel never lost it.

The devil's forces can't match God's authority.

Many times in my ministry I have seen people receive
healing and miracles hours, days, and weeks after praying for
them. God will do it!

17. Miracles Unknown

*Likewise the Spirit also helpeth our infirmities: for we
know not what we should pray for as we ought: but the
Spirit itself maketh intercession for us with groanings
which cannot be uttered. And he that searcheth the hearts
knoweth what is the mind of the Spirit, because he maketh
intercession for the saints according to the will of God.*

(Romans 8:26–27)

The Spirit intercedes for us in our healing.

Don't ever limit God to only what you or someone else
knows they need. God is so much smarter than we are. The
Holy Spirit will move on your behalf, even when you don't
realize it is happening.

18. Compassion Miracles

*And a certain man was there, which had an infirmity
thirty and eight years. When Jesus saw him lie, and knew*

that he had been now a long time in that case, he saith
unto him, Wilt thou be made whole? The impotent man
answered him, Sir, I have no man, when the water is
troubled, to put me into the pool: but while I am coming,
another steppeth down before me. Jesus saith unto him,
Rise, take up thy bed, and walk.   (John 5:5–8)

Jesus had compassion on someone who never would have
made it otherwise. When you start feeling the compassion for
hurting people, your ministry's anointing will increase.

19. Your Faith Needs to Seize a Miracle

You can't always sit back and wait for your miracle to
"maybe" occur. Sometimes you must aggressively, and always
in faith, seize your miracle:

+ A young deaf girl in India just put my hands on her ears
and was healed.

+ An Indian woman pushed through crowd to get me to
pray for her and was healed.

+ In Scripture, the woman with the issue of blood who
touched the garment of Jesus and received her healing.
(See Matthew 9:18–26; Mark 5:21–43; Luke 8:40–56.)

20. Ask God to Remove the Sickness from Your Home

If thou wilt diligently hearken to the voice of the LORD
thy God, and wilt do that which is right in his sight, and
wilt give ear to his commandments, and keep all his stat-
utes, I will put none of these diseases upon thee, which I
have brought upon the Egyptians: for I am the LORD *that*
healeth thee.   (Exodus 15:26)

One time in my home we had such a cold, cough, and throat sickness hit that every week, it seemed that one of us was passing on our bad cold to someone who had just recovered from it. I purposed one night to go before the Lord, telling the sickness, "No more!" I put my faith in Exodus 15:26, a promise of God to us that He will not put sickness on us and that He will heal us. I asked God to remove this sickness from our home for good…and He did!

21. Whosoever, Whatsoever Miracles

For verily I say unto you, That whosoever shall say unto this mountain, Be thou removed, and be thou cast into the sea; and shall not doubt in his heart, but shall believe that those things which he saith shall come to pass; he shall have whatsoever he saith. (Mark 11:23)

With a fig tree, Jesus demonstrated the power that exists behind the words we use. (See Mark 11:12–25.)

Jesus told everyone, *"Have faith in God"* (verse 22).

Tell your mountain to leave.

After getting this lesson of faith in my spirit, I have seen not only an increase in faith but also a miracle breakthrough in my life and ministry.

ABOUT THE AUTHOR

Pastor David Yanez is a leading faith and spiritual entrepreneur for the gospel, reaching the world through preaching, media, books, missions and broadcasting.

Pastor David "the Rev," has been preaching the gospel since he was sixteen. Innovative, resourceful, and technically savvy, he began doing overseas mission work in his early twenties as an associate evangelist with a ministry based in India reaching out to the 1.5 billion people in India and Asia. Today he continues his "in-person" mission work, reporting tremendous testimonies of salvation, healing, and deliverance in recent trips to India and Kenya.

In his early thirties, David began hosting the radio show *Midwatch with the Rev* and went on to found RevMedia Network, which reaches thousands of listeners and viewers worldwide.

The author of a number of books and founder of Rev Media Publishing, he recently released two Banner Publishing books: *Almost Out of Grace* and *The Recruit,* a book that includes personal stories of how God used him during his time in the U.S. Navy.

Here are the ministries he's founded and oversees:

+ **Revelation Ministries** operates David Yanez Ministries, a global missions and healing service ministry.

+ **RevMedia Network/RevMedia TV** is an IPTV broadcasting ministry that offers a platform for a wide variety of Christian teachers and preachers including *Midwatch with the Rev,* the daily radio and TV talk show Dr. Yanez hosts 11–12 A.M., CT.

+ **RevMedia Publishing** provides hard copy and digital books by a variety of faith-filled authors including many dynamic preachers and evangelists. It has currently eighteen authors and thirty-five titles.

+ **RevLife** is a global ministry created to provide food, medical care, clothing, education, and spiritual freedom to orphaned, traumatized, and neglected children.

With all God has entrusted to him, Dr. Yanez is a very down-to-earth man whose priorities lie close to home: "I'm first and foremost a child of God, a husband, and father. These are the relationships that matter most to me and for which I'm eternally thankful."

Dr. David and his wife live in the Houston, Texas area with their four children.

Author Website: www.davidyanezministries.net

Facebook: www.facebook.com/davidyanezministries

Book Website: whpub.me/igniteroffaith

Welcome to Our House!

We Have a Special Gift for You

It is our privilege and pleasure to share in your love of Christian books. We are committed to bringing you authors and books that feed, challenge, and enrich your faith.

To show our appreciation, we invite you to sign up to receive a specially selected **Reader Appreciation Gift,** with our compliments. Just go to the Web address at the bottom of this page.

God bless you as you seek a deeper walk with Him!

WE HAVE A GIFT FOR YOU. VISIT:

whpub.me/nonfictionthx

WHITAKER
HOUSE